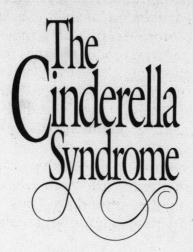

The Cinderella Syndrome

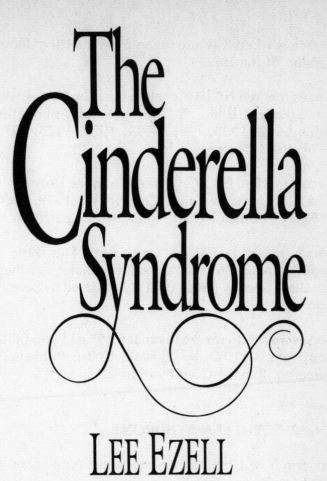

The Cinderella Syndrome

Lee Ezell

HARVEST HOUSE PUBLISHERS
Eugene, Oregon 97402

THE CINDERELLA SYNDROME

Copyright © 1985 by Harvest House Publishers
Eugene, Oregon 97402

Library of Congress Catalog Card Number 85-60122
ISBN 0-89081-475-9

Printed in the United States of America.

ACKNOWLEDGMENT

As Lela Gilbert's nimble little fingers ran over this manuscript, she unscrambled all its tangles and (without any magic dust) transformed it into the helpful book which follows.

Thank you, Lela!

*To Hal—not exactly Prince Charming—
but a charming husband,
who's a prince of a guy!*

FOREWORD

If ever there was a Cinderella in search of a Prince Charming, it was me.

If ever someone wanted to live happily ever after, it was me.

I was full of fantasies and fairy tales until I found out that life is real and many of our experiences don't have happy endings.

Lee Ezell has written this book for people like me, and how I wish I'd had it years ago, when I was still searching for a fairy godmother behind every bush.

Whatever Lee speaks or writes she does with her unique style and humor. As a member of our CLASS seminar staff, she keeps us all laughing and brightens the corners where we are. I know her witty words will brighten your corner of the world as she shows you how to free yourself from the fetters of the past, how to live content in whatever state you are, and how to look forward with hope to the future.

What more could you ask?

—Florence Littauer

CONTENTS

Chapter One

Long Ago And Far Away

I awakened Monday morning with a strange sense that something wasn't quite right. Drowsily I tried to summon my senses. What was the trouble? I rolled over to look at the clock. Pain cut through my right arm. Then I remembered.

The night before my father had lost control of himself—again. My sisters and I had in varying degrees felt the fury of his belt and his fists. As usual, my mother had received the worst of it. She always tried to spare us injury during his beatings. And she always paid for it.

But today was a school day. There would be no recuperation time, bruised though I was. I would just have to locate a long-sleeved shirt in my meager wardrobe—something to hide the black-and-blue evidence. And I would leave our unhappy household behind, making the best of my world away from home.

I rummaged through my closet. There wasn't an article of clothing there that hadn't first belonged to one of my two older sisters. Since I was in the middle, I got things before they were totally threadbare. Brand-new, store-bought items were few and far between.

A gray skirt. A navy-blue turtleneck. I quickly pulled them on, brushed my teeth, and ran a brush through my short brown hair. *Won't it ever grow?* I grumbled silently. Smiling a feeble smile at the mirror, I thanked my stars that there was school today. Anything to get out of the house! I grabbed my books and violin case and slammed the front door behind me.

Racing down our street toward the streetcar was such a familiar practice that I barely noticed the plain, unappealing row houses. Their dreary brick facades weren't the least bit flattered by the faded brown patch of grass that was allotted each one. This token "front yard" was barely ten feet square. And it was a rare residence that added the color of a potted flower or the freshness of a coat of paint to its dull decor.

If a city planner had found his way to our West Philadelphia neighborhood he would have no doubt, declared it a "depressed area." It wasn't exactly urban blight. It was just hopeless.

For a kid like me to go to school with parent-

inflicted bruises was nothing special. The Mac-
Farland family down the street got it much worse
than we did. Their dad beat them up at least once
a week. And he didn't even have to be drunk to
do it—just mad.

In spite of all the sadness, I had found a life
of my own there in the City of Brotherly Love.
Music was my escape. I had played the violin for
ten of my 17 years. I had sung in choirs and
musicals since seventh grade.And I had been a
regular on Dick Clark's American Bandstand TV
show for 2½ years.

Three afternoons a week I would jump on the
subway after school and head for the hall where
Chubby Checker, Frankie Avalon, and Connie
Francis were familiar faces. Theirs were only a
few of the names in my autograph book! And by
now I didn't have to wait in line outside. I just
waved hello to the guard.

"Hey, Lee, how's it goin'?" he would respond.
Opening the door, he would grin and let me
inside.

The prettiest girls who were "regulars" got free
clothes from the famous department stores in the
area. They danced in them on camera, and when
the credits rolled, the stores got free advertising.
As for me, I was more than content to rock the
afternoons away in my secondhand apparel. The
glamour of being part of all this "Sixties Action"
was reward enough.

But the sixties weren't just a time for happy
white kids to vote on new tunes in front of television cameras. There was racial unrest from coast

to coast. Three years later the Watts riots would engulf blocks and blocks of Los Angeles in flames.

Understandably, the blacks in Philly weren't too impressed with the "white only" rules of Dick Clark's afternoon rock-and-roll celebration. One evening I waited for the subway, shivering a little in the late fall cold. Suddenly a strange dread began to chill me even more. It was triggered by shouts and screams moving toward me from an unseen source.

All at once, around a corner came an army of angry young blacks. They were armed with bottles and stones. And I was a likely target with my pale face. Fortunately I escaped on a timely subway train. It whisked me away from the scene of a soon-to-be bloody confrontation, one of many I was to experience.

I rode alone toward the streetcar connection which would eventually deliver me close to home. My knees were rubbery. My hands shook uncontrollably in my lap. Another close call. I knew it. And it wouldn't be the last. No 16-year-old girl could ride around beneath the streets of a tough city like that without a few near misses. That night I felt helplessly alone.

But throughout my teenage years, I had no one to travel with me. I didn't confide in friends— why drag them into my troubles? And my sisters were as busy as I was, trying to stay alive. They weren't interested in my worries. They had enough of their own.

It wasn't hard to name the culprit in our family. The effect that alcohol had on my dad was both dramatic and dangerous. Mother drew further and further away from us as his condition worsened. She worked day and night to keep money coming in for bare necessities. She was exhausted and increasingly depressed.

By trade, Father was a housepainter. But his brush seldom left our house. He spent most of his hours in the basement, staring at the pornography with which he had papered the walls and ceiling. When he wasn't lost in his own thoughts there, he would sit on the flat roof of the house, staring at other sights that only he could appreciate.

Outside of occasional neighborhood card games, there was little mirth in our home. But I did laugh uproariously during my favorite homemade diversion—"Roach Race." A couple of us would gather in the kitchen and perch on the chairs. Someone would flip the lights out. After two minutes they were switched back on, and the one who jumped down and squashed the most roaches won!

Mother ruled her brood of daughters with the iron hand that befitted her German and English heritage. She had always kept matters short and direct from day one. Each girl was provided with only one name made up of three letters. Hence we were known as Zoe, Ann, Lee, Kay, and Sue Kinney.

My mother's determined spirit made the difference in our lives. She worked hard and long to provide for our needs. She did her best to protect us. And despite her stern discipline, she always encouraged us to pursue our talents.

In those days, neighborhoods were less transient than they are now. We grew up in the same house where Mother was raised. And our street was a melting pot of nationalities. An Italian family lived on our right, an Irish family on our left, a German family across the street. I absorbed the characteristics of all these cultures. And through my friendships there I gained a love for language and ethnic tradition.

Religion was represented among the neighbors in variety too. Each family taught me something different about God. From the Catholics I learned that religion was fun when you were older—then you got to go to wakes and big weddings! And Catholic kids went to parochial school in crisp uniforms—no hand-me-downs. This seemed very prestigious to me!

From the Jews I learned about religious holidays and ceremonies with hard-to-pronounce names. Their faith didn't seem to invite converts. And worse yet, they didn't celebrate Christmas.

From the lone Christian on the block, I learned that these folks never played cards. They refused to wear lipstick. And their children couldn't play on Sunday. (It was apparently all right to sit on the porch and *envy* the other kids, but *playing* was a sin.)

Our family faithfully attended our own neighborhood sanctuary—a grand, musty old church. *This must be a holy place*, I thought as I gazed at the saints peering down at me from their stained-glass windows. Here in "God's house" I could visit Him on Sundays, whisper my sins to Him, tell Him I was sorry, and promise to come back next week. Sometimes the minister mentioned the Bible. But it certainly wasn't offered as a book for personal use.

There was a great loneliness in my life during those years. It seemed to me that "someone" was missing. Was it a boyfriend? A better parent? Maybe a close friend would fill the void. I was a whirlwind of activity. But I was always running— away from pain, from rejection, from punishment. My life was geared toward escape. And with rare exceptions I was a real Houdini when it came to keeping out of the line of fire.

Yet the sad emptiness persisted. My love for music and song may have inadvertently compounded the problem. Love songs have a way of sounding like the "man I love" could change the world and make everything all right.

Sometimes as I shivered on the brink of terror in the shadowy subway, I imagined a strong, beautiful boyfriend at my side. He would protect me from the invisible enemies that seemed to lurk everywhere. The dangers were no figment of my imagination—just the boyfriend!

Emptiness. Loneliness. Fear. And a vague hope for "something or someone" who would change the world for me. These were my innermost feelings. And I carried them with me one night to a strange new event in the Philadelphia civic calendar.

"Ever heard of a preacher named Billy Graham?" I had asked my mother curiously the night before.

"Are you kidding?" She had snapped back. "That holy roller?"

"Three of us are going to hear him tonight at the Convention Center. We *were* going to play pinochle, but we can't find a fourth, so we decided to go hear this guy for kicks."

There was a massive crowd at the arena— larger than I would ever have guessed. And I couldn't help but smile at the beautiful music that swelled from the enormous choir. It was all so big!

A heavyset, unimpressive-looking black woman made her weary way to the microphone. She walked with some difficulty. *What is she doing up there?* I wondered.

Then she began to sing.

> Why should I feel discouraged?
> Why should the shadows come?
> Why should my heart be lonely
> And long for heaven and home?

I vaguely recalled the name Ethel Waters from my study of musical comedy and theater. But to hear her sing those particular words at that point in my life—the effect on me was devastating. "His eye is on the sparrow, and I *know* He watches me." Tears poured down my cheeks. I turned my face so my friends wouldn't see. My heart was pounding.

Billy Graham's message was just as profound

as the song. For the first time in my life I heard that God cared about *me* personally. He loved me. He could live inside me and always be with me.

These were astounding, life-changing ideas in my young mind. Would Jesus really ride the subway with me? Would He protect me? Could I talk to Him about my problems?

Like hundreds of others, as the service ended, I made my way to the front of the reverent crowd. The spiritual concepts weren't too clear in my mind. I only knew I had never before surrendered my life to Christ—and this was my moment.

My friends left me there, so I found my way to the subway alone. I felt I had added something clean, something beautiful, to my life. Would my world be transformed now? Would everything be different when I reached my home? What would God do for me?

High on hope, I rushed to the familiar front door and threw it open. The first thing that met my eyes was my father's slouched, drunken form. *Well*, I thought dryly, *some things even God doesn't mess with*.

I was disappointed, yes. The "magic" I had always looked for hadn't happened. But I persisted in my new relationship to God. I wrote for the materials the Billy Graham Crusade counselor had promised. I filled out the Bible study materials and mailed them faithfully to Minneapolis. And the more I learned, the more a new strength began to grow deep inside me. A new "independence" was emerging—not *from* God, but *with* God. However, my troubles were far from over.

Just before high school graduation, my father flew into one of his most violent rages ever. He began to beat us with his homemade cat-o'-nine-tails. By that time two of my sisters had married and left. Of those girls who remained, and Mother, not one of us escaped visible wounds.

The next morning I confronted my sisters and Mom. "I'm leaving after graduation. I'm going to live with Zoe (my oldest sister) in California. Anyone who wants to join me is welcome. But I've *had* it. I'm getting out of here."

As it turned out, Mother joined both my sisters and me as we made our way on the bus to sunny California. (Sadly, we left my father to his pornography and his booze.) Zoe and her husband lived near San Francisco. We would try to make a life for ourselves close by.

The four of us settled into a cramped, colorless apartment in the busy Bay Area. Soon I landed my first legitimate secretarial job. All seemed to be going as well as possible for a battered quartet of out-of-state females.

Then, one afternoon at work, I was approached by a man whom I had only seen there only a handful of times. He forced his overweight person upon me. Threatened me. Raped me.

I was devastated. It would take years for all the complicated pieces of this new puzzle to fall into place for me. But my emotionally scarred sisters and mother didn't seem capable of dealing with yet another crisis. In the confused aftermath, it was best for my family that I leave the area.

So I fled to Southern California alone. There I made a new life for myself. After some recuperation, I spent a year in Bible school. I took a variety of jobs in churches, doing any and every kind of secretarial work. Eventually I joined the staff as a Bible teacher.

One day Bill Morgan, my boss, confided, "We are seriously considering relocating!"

"Where are you going?" I asked, feeling a little frightened by the sudden announcement.

Bill smiled. He knew how radical his next statement would be. "Florida!" he simply said.

"Florida!" I was at a loss for further words. But in the days to come, I prayed and sought the will of God in my life. Maybe a new set of surroundings would be good for me. Maybe Florida would be the place to which my prince would come. Another adventure? Why not!

In a roundabout way, I was right. My prince did show up in Florida. But he wasn't the prince I had in mind. And, as it turned out, I had a lot to learn about Cinderella!

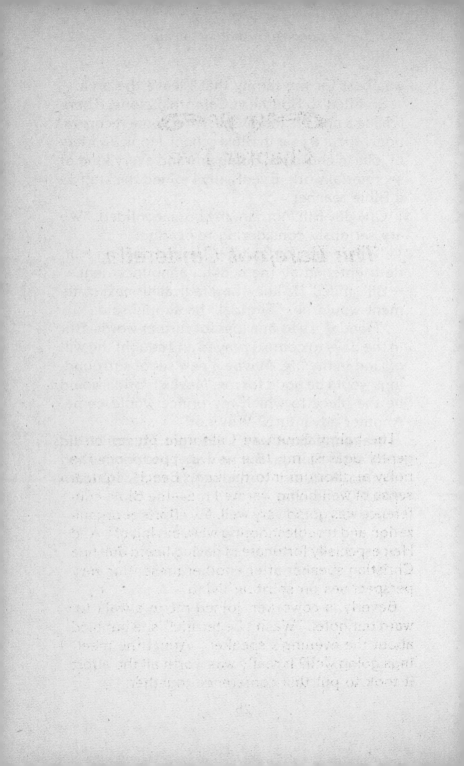

Chapter Two

The Barefoot Cinderella

The balmy Southern California breeze blew gently against my face as I stepped from the noisy auditorium into the Long Beach night. A sense of well-being warmed me—the Bible conference was going very well. My efforts at organization and troubleshooting were paying off. And I felt especially fortunate in having heard one fine Christian speaker after another presenting new perspectives on spiritual living.

Beverly, a coworker, joined me in a walk toward our hotel. "Wasn't he terrific!" she bubbled about the evening's speaker. "Aren't the meetings going well? It really was worth all the effort it took to put this conference together!"

I laughed at Beverly. She was always enthusi-
astic—and here in Long Beach she was like a
butterfly, happily flitting about, assisting in
all the details that made things run smoothly
for the conference attendees. I started to kid
her about her eternal optimism when a round-
faced man greeted us. "How are you two lovely
Florida ladies enjoying this California weather?"
He smiled and continued, "Listen, I want to
invite you and Bill and all the Florida team
to my home after the closing meeting tomorrow
night."

We both recognized the man as Hal Ezell, the
director of this West Coast Bible conference.

"Oh, thanks!" Beverly responded quickly. "Of
course we'd *love* to come."

"Well, there's only one hitch." Hal paused
thoughtfully. "I'll have to check and see how my
wife's feeling tomorrow, before we make definite
arrangements. She's been a little under the
weather and she may not feel up to having company. But I'm sure she'll be better by then!" he
concluded with a confident grin.

"Just let Bill know," I told Hal. "The staff is
planning to spend tomorrow evening together,
so whatever you two decide will be fine with
us."

Bill Morgan, our boss, was a well-known Bible
teacher from Florida. A day or two before, Bill
had asked us to pray for Hal's wife. "Wanda has
rheumatoid arthritis and can't play the organ for
our meetings. Hal seems to expect her to improve
any day, though."

I had heard of Wanda Shows Ezell before. She was a Christian musician who had performed on television from time to time until her occasional bouts with painful joints became more frequent and severe. I knew she was very talented and had wondered absently why a woman with such gifts should be stricken with a handicap like arthritis.

The next morning Beverly and I rushed into a crowded coffee shop to grab a bite of breakfast. Hal Ezell was in a booth with two pretty young girls. "Hello, there!" He greeted us cheerfully. "Say, tell Bill I'm afraid we're going to have to take a raincheck on our evening at my place. Wanda's still feeling pretty bad." We murmured our regrets.

Then Hal continued brightly, with a glance at his companions, "I'd like to introduce you to a couple of very special young ladies—Pamela and Sandra, my daughters. Girls, these two are from Florida—Beverly and. . .what was your name again?"

"Lee." I smiled at the two pretty faces. Pam and Sandi (at 10 and 13) seemed unusually quiet and reserved for their ages. "Maybe they're worried about their mom," I remarked to Bev later on.

Two weeks passed. Back at work in my office in Florida, one of the secretaries mentioned a phone call she had received earlier that day. "Lee? Remember Hal Ezell? The man who organized the Long Beach Bible conference? His wife died this morning!"

"Died!" I felt a shudder of shock. "How could she die? All she had was arthritis!"

"Well, it wasn't arthritis after all. It was something called 'lupus.' Ever heard of it? She was in the last stages and didn't know it when they took her to the emergency room. She was dead nine hours later!"

"Those poor little girls," I said, half to myself as I left the room, tears stinging my eyes. Back in the office, I sat transfixed. The news had really shaken me. How could such a terrible thing happen?

Later that week my California friend who had attended the funeral sent me the little booklet from the memorial service.

Sitting on the side of my bed, ready to turn the light out and fall asleep, I examined the little blue remembrance with Wanda's name, date of birth, and all the usual information printed soberly inside. "Those *poor* little girls of hers. And poor Hal." I lay down anxious for sleep. Instead half-a-dozen hours passed quietly, and my eyes never closed.

The next morning some of us were waiting for a meeting to begin, seated around a conference table. Dick commented, "You guys think it's hard on Hal Ezell losing a wife? Do you realize that this is the *second* wife he's lost in the last seven years? After nine years of happy marriage his first wife, Helen, died of a brain tumor. And she was only 30 years old. You know, those girls are her daughters, not Wanda's."

I could hardly believe my ears. What a tragedy! As the days went by I found myself thinking of Hal Ezell more and more. Those thoughts gradually became a problem to me—almost an obsession. "At least it isn't physical attraction," I comforted myself wryly. "As far as I was concerned, Hal Ezell was not exactly my idea of "Prince Charming." More puzzling was the fact that my feelings weren't especially romantic, either. The last involvement I would ever have dreamed of would have been with an older man, twice happily married—a man with two heartbroken daughters. None of that sounded like romance to me!

Yet I couldn't escape the awareness of that sorrowing California family. I waited one evening until everyone had left and desperately rummaged through the files, searching for a Long Beach Bible conference brochure. I couldn't even remember what Hal Ezell looked like, yet he was always in my thoughts.

At last I went to Bill Morgan and his wife for help. I poured out my confusion to them. "Why am I obsessed with thoughts of this man I can hardly remember? He's constantly on my mind! Where do I go from here?"

Bill and Judy seemed mildly amused, but they were kind and took the time to reassure me I wasn't cracking up. "This *could* be from the Lord." Bill studied me intently as I stepped out the front door toward my car. "Had you thought about that?"

"Thanks, but no thanks," I mumbled. "You

could *die* from such a blessing!" I thought to myself, quoting Golde from *Fiddler on the Roof.*

While driving home I thought of nothing but my strange fixation on this character Hal Ezell. I was 28 years old. I had a terrific job and a great life. Even though I was considered to be verging on "spinsterhood," I didn't care if I ever got married. I wasn't really looking for a man— mainly because I figured that no man was looking for me. Furthermore, if I *were* to marry it certainly wouldn't be to a twice-widowed man with two young daughters! God had a better idea for *me*—of that I was sure.

It wasn't long before Hal Ezell arrived in Florida for a meeting with my boss to set up another Christian Growth conference. When he called our office he somehow found himself talking to me. "Maybe we can have dinner sometime or something. I guess I'm single again whether I want to be or not."

When I saw him the next day, he had on white patent leather shoes and a white belt, and strongly resembled a big spender from the West Coast. By contrast, I was a "holy old maid" garbed in modest gray. In short, I didn't like the looks of him! So why were my thoughts always with him?

The following evening, during our dinner together, a brief period of silence fell between the clink of silver and the murmur of conversation. As if on cue, I plunged bravely into my story. I told Hal how he had possessed my thoughts for weeks. I told him I was confused and be-

wildered by my own ambivalence. He told me
that we were from two different worlds. How right
he was!

We disagreed on so many points in our very
first real conversation! We knew that we were
totally different and unsuitable for each other.
Yet by the time Hal Ezell left Florida, we both
knew that it was God's will that we be married.

My first fantasy of a handsome, carefree young
bachelor who would marry *me*—his first and
only love—was abruptly set aside. Instead, I
found myself reveling in the love of another
prince, this one the man of God's choosing.
We had a gorgeous wedding and a marvelous
honeymoon. Not surprisingly, I began to develop
a new dream—of a life lived happily ever after.
And in actuality it started out just that way.

My prince had money. A house. A car. Real
estate. He was accomplished in business. And he
wanted me! Surely no cloud would shadow our
years together. After all, hadn't this poor man
had enough trouble? It was time he had some
happy years. I would be the one to share his newfound happiness. And the girls were a delightful
bonus! No diapers, no delivery. Just two lovely
girls.

At the outset I thought we would share a storybook life. Finally this "Maria" had found her Captain Von Trapp, and she and his children would
dance and sing together merrily. Isn't that the
way it was supposed to be?

Soon I had the rude awakening. I had spent
more time preparing for my wedding than I had

for my marriage! (Florence Littauer has aptly described this common malady in her book titled *After Every Wedding Comes a Marriage*.)

The first morning of our honeymoon, Hal awoke early. As he reached across me to phone the girls, I thought, *This isn't right! Isn't he supposed to be making up poetry now, like Dr. Zhivago? Shouldn't he be at least sweeping me off my feet, carrying me up a winding staircase like Rhett Butler?*

I had somehow imagined that "married life" would mean waking up fresh every morning, tying my nightie around my tiny waist, and rushing off to make a gourmet breakfast for my Prince.

It wasn't long before harsh, bitter words cut through my fantasy like a dagger. "I will *never* call you Mom!" "I will never love *anyone* again!" One moment would find me stricken with sorrow and self-pity. The next moment I would be overwhelmed with compassion for two terrified little girls who had lost two mothers. Who could blame them for their anger?

Nevertheless, time and time again in those first rocky years of parenting we would have the kind of emotional eruptions that often occur in step-family living. "I don't care! I don't have to obey her! She's not my mother. And besides, I don't like her!"

One thing would lead to another, and before long all four of us would be in tears. It was through repeated sessions like this, crying and praying with the girls, that healing began to take place. But the struggle at the time was overwhelming. All three members of my new family wanted desperately to freely love again, yet each one had to experience emotional healing. That would take a while, for there is no substitute for the passing of time.

Hal was not without times of moodiness and depression. "I should have married a nice *divorced* man," I secretly informed my mirror one day. "At least a divorcee *wants* to be single. This guy was happy but struck out twice. And now I feel like nothing but a pinch hitter!"

We argued. We stormed. Hal wanted a replacement for two sweet Christian ladies. He was understandably afraid to love. I was outspoken, unlike my predecessors. Hal seemed to want me to submit without discussion. One day I desperately flew off to San Francisco alone, leaving the whole mess behind me. Would it ever work? The only thing that had kept me going was my absolute certainty that God had clearly drawn the two of us together. There was no doubt in my mind about *that*. After a few days, and many tears, I returned to Hal, determined to work at being married again.

It seemed to me that Hal's former wives were always present. One evening as we dressed to go out, Hal said, "Don't wear that jacket; wear your black coat."

"What black coat?"

"You know—the long one."

"But I don't *have* a black coat!"

"Oh . . . never mind."

Another day Sandi casually remarked, "How come you never make that great chicken casserole anymore?"

"What chicken casserole?"

"You know...oh...never mind."

It didn't take long for my "happily-ever-after" fantasy to be forever dashed. I was dealing with a very bruised family, to whom I was little more than a stranger. Worse yet, I was separated from my own dear friends and a sunny life in Florida. It was a time of suffering and lonely tears.

Nevertheless, I was a fighter, and my determined personality began to serve me well.

During those first months together, in order to break the somber spell that had fallen upon our house, I employed my two favorite techniques—music and imagination. Singing songs was like breathing to me, and I taught Pam and Sandi how to write new lyrics to old ones. Together we acted out "radio skits" into the cassette recorder. We produced puppet shows for the church and minidramas for Dad.

Slowly but steadily I felt I earned the girls' respect. They began to very naturally call me "Mom." Even more slowly love put out tiny, fragile shoots in their battered hearts.

Meanwhile, within me, a love for them began to grow that exceeded even my most optimistic expectations. With all respect for their natural mother, I can honestly say that today I love them as though they were my very own birth-daughters.

My marriage proved to be more difficult than my newfound motherhood. Without meaning to do so, I had molded a role for Hal that went beyond his place as my lover and partner. Without even informing him, I was depending on him for my happiness. He was my provider, protector, and promised one, wasn't he? Well, then, wasn't it up to him to make me happy? What had happened to the marriage that I thought was "God's perfect will"? I managed to convince myself that it belonged in the second category, "God's permissive will." This would, of course, make it easier for me to end it.

Under that kind of pressure, Hal couldn't help but fail. And I became disappointed, disenchanted, and disillusioned. Gradually, without knowing it myself, I had begun the long climb up the winding staircase into the "fairytale tower."

My imagination, so useful in providing ideas to entertain and woo my two new daughters, began to invent new dreams to replace my lost ones. I imagined how much better our marriage would have been if I were Hal's first and only love. I visualized raising the girls as their natural mother (a trick of the mind common to stepmothers!). I speculated about how much better a wife I would have been if I had grown up in a different environment. I spun strand after strand of a sticky web that began to strangle the simple joys of daily living and to imprison me in a fictitious, impossible dreamworld.

There is something extraordinarily deceptive about daydreaming. In a sense it seems like a harmless pastime, able to transport us from our mundane existence into any paradise we can envision. But in fact daydreams often make us miserable within the daily effort of life because they *breed dissatisfaction.*

In the early years of my marriage to Hal, I felt rejection because he didn't seem to accept me as my outspoken, communicative self. On one occasion, when I tried to explain to him Tim LaHaye's perspective of the "sanguine" personality (which was me) versus "phlegmatic" (him), he was horrified! He thought this kind of categorizing was tantamount to saying "I'm a Virgo and you're a Libra—so what do you expect?" Of course I consider astrological explanations as being dangerous ground, but as far as I was concerned, the temperament titles fit us all too well!

Besides my high expectations for Hal and my unrealistic fantasies, the heart of our problem lay in the fact that neither of us had a healthy understanding of what submission in marriage really meant. I felt I had to fit a "Total Woman" image. (Instead, I totaled out!) Hal was convinced of a hard-line policy on wife-husband submission (i.e. dictatorship). We both thought the biblical definition of submission was something like "barefoot and pregnant; doormat."

In this stance of "submersion" rather than true biblical "submission," I required myself to suppress my own true feelings, opinions, and desires. Without expression, I tried to quietly go along with the program, attempting to make no waves.

Have you ever tried to hold a beach ball under the water? Sooner or later it will pop up, out of control. I frequently encountered circumstances in which I could no longer keep my mouth shut! At the same time, I felt guilty and wrong whenever I expressed an opposing viewpoint to the "powers that be." We seemed to disagree about almost everything!

(I was comforted when someone reminded me that if two agree all the time on everything, one of them is not necessary!)

Eventually we discovered that we had adopted a faulty interpretation of Scripture. Our perspective was *causing separation* between us rather than bringing us into a better relationship. My discovery of author Betty Coble's definition of biblical submission changed our lives. She defines it as a wife becoming a "participating follower." That sounded better to me than submersion *or* suppression! This wife does not follow blindly without participation, nor does she assertively state her opinions and feelings without a submitted attitude.

Perhaps most important of all, I learned that communication is really the avenue for a wife's submission. When 1 Peter 3:1 recommends that "wives submit yourselves to your own husbands," it doesn't mean that we can't speak up!

Within these newly defined terms, I began

to feel the freedom which God intended. I realized that submission was not a *value* word but
simply an *organizational* word. Together, Hal and
I relaxed a little. And I began to realize that my
happiness really wasn't his responsibility after
all.

I recall the night we sat together in the spa, just
the two of us. I took a deep breath and made my
"big statement."

"Honey? I have some good news!"

My phlegmatic, never-ruffled husband mumbled, "Yeah?"

"I have finally realized that all this time I've
been holding you responsible for my happiness.
And I want to take that load off you tonight! I've
come to see that God holds *me* responsible for
carving my own happiness, and I just want you
to know that I'm relieving you of that responsibility!" (I did it! I said it!)

My big statement didn't seem very important
to Hal at the time, but over a period of weeks and
months he recognized a change in me, and in
turn began to feel freer, less burdened. Before
long our marriage grew stronger. Today I realize
that there is no one on earth with whom I could
be more happily married.

After attending a course for Christian wives,
I became so inspired that I signed up to take it
again. I could see the impact it was having in my
own home. Soon Hal and I began to practice new
principles in conversation. In sharing. In loving.
The more I learned and grew, the more chal-
lenged I became.

Soon I learned how to teach the course. For two years I was an instructor. And as I studied and listened and shared with so many women, our marriage was transformed. Hal grew more confident, less afraid to listen. I became more independent with regard to my own emotional stability. Old scars from the past began to heal in Hal's life and in the lives of Pam and Sandi. And newly torn wounds were miraculously mended too, for we all were discovering how to live together in a more honest, biblical, life-giving way.

The answers to our problems had been available in the Bible all along. Now, with the Lord's help, we had begun to appropriate them. How neat to discover that they were not burdensome, but freeing!

Scriptures began to fall in place for me as I found that I had to work with the Lord more intimately in learning contentment in whatever state I was in (Philippians 4:11).

It was deeply satisfying to sense what the Lord wanted from me, and I enjoyed such an inner sense of gratification when I would obey. In doing so, I began to respect myself far more. Galatians 6:4 encouraged me that I was on the right track.

> But let each one examine his own work, and then he will have rejoicing in himself alone, and not in another (NKJV).

Perhaps most surprising of all was the ministry

that God opened up for me. The course I was teaching became much more adapted to my own experience and my perception of women's problems and needs. To my delight, invitations for me to speak came more frequently. It was humbling to find that when I spoke, I found myself counseling—and soon dozens of women became hundreds of women. (I guess I have the kind of face people like to confess into.)

The more I listened, the more I heard the same familiar tale. Cinderella was forever "*waiting* for the glass slipper." Sleeping Beauty was forever *waiting* for the right kiss. And somehow, the forever-after never came. We had all believed the pretty stories, and we had all been disappointed! I gave the problem I perceived a new name— "The Cinderella Syndrome." I recognized it again and again.

Soon I learned that the secular feminists had their own solutions to the problem. I rejected the conclusions I found offered in Colette Dowling's book titled *The Cinderella Complex.* While the author seemed to correctly analyze a woman's dependency problem, she failed to offer any viable, godly solutions, for finding contentment.

But what about us Christian women? Can we find answers of our own? Where, for example, do we draw the line between waiting on the Lord and waiting for the glass slipper? Is there a balance between dreams-that-never-will-come-true and true faith that a miracle will eventually happen?

How can we survive in the midst of truly crummy circumstances? Can we flee our fairytale towers, run back down the winding staircase, and find true contentment in the here-and-now?

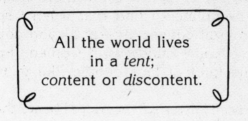

All the world lives
in a *tent*;
*c*ontent or *dis*content.

Chapter Three

The Cinderella Syndrome

Diana's exquisite hat framed her lovely smile and softly windblown hair. The young couple waved joyfully, her glittering sapphire-and-diamond ring catching the sunlight as they drove away. Like a vast backdrop, millions of tiny flags fluttered and a roar of cheers echoed in the streets of London. The royal honeymoon had begun!

Everyone loves a Cinderella story. People around the world fixed their delighted eyes upon their television sets as pretty Lady Diana Spencer was transformed into the glamorous Princess of Wales. Her storybook romance with Prince Charles dominated the papers and captivated our

hearts. What little girl wouldn't dream of growing up to be just as beautiful, bright, and blessed
as Diana!

To the relief of all of us, she and her prince
seem to be living together with some semblance
of happiness. But whatever happened to Cinderella, Snow White, Sleeping Beauty, or any of
those other winsome princesses *after* their
respective wedding ceremonies? With the excep-
tion of Charles and Di, every "happily ever after"
story seems to end with the wedding march.

Before she found her prince, Cinderella had a
miserable existence. Yet in her heart, she kept
a secret hope that someday things would change.
Who can forget the night her mean stepsisters
and stepmother went to the ball, leaving poor little Cinderella to weep and sweep?

Miraculously, her fairy godmother appeared,
waved the famous wand and whisked Cinderella
off to the ball, where she lost her glass slipper.

Later on, as the prince searched his kingdom
for that special size five foot, he fell more deeply
in love with Cinderella. Nothing could dim his
devotion.

At last he found her! He swept her off her tiny
feet and placed her on his white steed, and together they rode off into the sunset—a perfect
ending to a delightful story.

As much as we've all exulted in the pleasant
tale, we must be honest enough to ask ourselves,
"Does life *really* offer such fairytale solutions?"

*The "Cinderella Syndrome" convinces us that
happiness was yesterday and will be someday but*

definitely is not now. Happiness is either lost in the past or is due to arrive "later on," as soon as certain anticipated events occur. *Then* we can be content. *Now* we are the victims of circumstance.

This fairytale mentality holds us captive in its castle and prevents us from enjoying *today.* It's a kind of self-imposed prison. Yet, unfortunately, the Cinderella promise is made to us every day in books, songs, and the media.

Did you see the television movie about a 40-year-old wife who was sure her happiness rested with her 27-year-old tennis instructor? Naturally *he* really understood her. She left her husband of 20 years for this "macho man" of the tennis courts who promised he would "make her happy." Guess what—he didn't.

The story has been told time and again. It's recounted to little girls who see marriage as the answer. It's related to little boys with success as the savior. In fact, nearly all "happy-ending" stories for children or adults offer very unreal answers to very difficult problems. God is usually left out or replaced by an imaginary someone with magic dust in his pocket.

Women suffer severely from fantasy thinking, but men are not immune either. Many a young man sells his soul for financial security. Many a husband reaches out for greener pastures of youth and sex. In real life, one discovers just as many weeds and snails on one side of the marital fence as on the other. Nevertheless, the illusion is very convincing.

The Cinderella Syndrome frustrates its victims. Under its spell, we are either hoping for things that were never meant to happen or reaching for dreams whose fulfillments are marred with disappointment.

Proverbs 13:12 tells it like it is: "Hope deferred makes the heart sick" (NKJV). In modern language, sick hearts are depressed hearts, and once depression begins, it's not easily dispelled. When we frivolously spend our hopes buying faulty merchandise, our hearts grow tired and ill. We who are inclined toward Cinderella thinking must yank its aggressive roots from the soil of our hearts before it chokes the goodness of life from our gardens.

Before you start weeding *your* flowerbed, take a close look at what's growing there. Sometimes weeds don't look like weeds at first glance. Why not go to work on the following questionnaire? See if any of these symptoms apply to you.

SYMPTOMS QUESTIONNAIRE

(Confidential; between patient and Great Physician)

1. I am NOT waiting for any fantasies to come true:

    _____true   _____false

(If you mark "false," that means you ARE waiting.)

2. I can describe myself as someone who is satisfied with her current circumstances:

    _____true   _____false

3. If my job/career never changes, I'm satisfied:
   _____true   _____false
4. I'm convinced I married the right person:
   _____true   _____false
5. If I never marry, that's fine:
   _____true   _____false
6. I don't have any "if only . . ." dreams:
   _____true   _____false
7. I can say of myself that I live in the present, not in the future or the past:
   _____true   _____false
8. My parents (or the people who raised me) were happy and contented during my childhood:
   _____true   _____false
9. Most of the dreams I held have come true:
   _____true   _____false
10. I see a difference between a dream and a goal:
    _____true   _____false

Scoring the questionnaire is easy. Count the number of answers you marked *false*. If you marked three or less false, you're pretty healthy. You might just suffer from a slight touch of fantasy thinking now and then, but who doesn't? If you marked three or more, it's probably time to get busy. By the way, don't feel too bad if you find that your score wasn't the greatest.

Plenty of famous people probably would have flunked the questionnaire. I think of Mary and

Martha (friends of Jesus from Bethany), who were troubled with "if only" thoughts. As recorded in John 11, when Jesus arrived at their dead brother's tomb, they told Him that He was too late. "If only you had been here . . ." They thought their chance for happiness had slipped past them.

Jesus replied, "Lazarus will rise again." And Martha agreed, "I know he will rise again in the resurrection at the last day." Besides "if only," Martha was sure the answer to her problems lay in the future "someday." Jesus did away with both of these fantasies by turning to the tomb of Lazarus and calling "Come forth!" Then and there Jesus showed us all that our possibilities for joy are not in the past or the future but very much in the present moment. Why? Because of His power!

"Well," you might argue, "fairy tales often have miraculous conclusions too. So what's the difference?" With God, all things *are* possible. But Paul also said, "Godliness *with contentment* is great gain" (1 Timothy 6:6 NKJV).

The opposite of fairytale thinking is contentment. Yet this most desirable state of peace and serenity eludes many of us. Why? What are the archenemies of contentment?

The Disillusioning Past

Patsy stared at her reflection in the hallway mirror. She had just pulled the last roller out of her hair, and she stopped long enough to take stock of her face. What she saw made her feel a surge of annoyance. "I'm getting *old*," she muttered under her breath as she grabbed her handbag and raced toward the door. She tripped over a pair of Billy's filthy jeans, left carelessly in the hall. Steadying herself, she blurted, "Like father, like son! Can't you ever *pick up your junk*?"

"So what, Mom?" Billy's adolescent voice cracked as he defiantly glared at Patsy from his bed. "I'll leave my clothes anywhere I want!"

As she drove toward her doctor's office, late for her appointment, anger seethed inside her. Sure, Jim was a hardworking, good provider as husbands go. They would never do without. But he did nothing at home to help Patsy out. She had never seen the man lift a dish from the table and carry it into the kitchen—not once in 17 years. He had never taken out the trash. He had yet to pick up a single article of his scattered clothing.

His sons were exactly like him—all four of them. The eldest, Billy, had recently begun to talk roughly to her. Patsy reminded herself, "He's acting like I did at his age." She too had been rebellious. And her early adventures with drugs and sex had led to one of the heaviest aches in her heart—an abortion at age 19.

As miserable a time as she had had in somehow raising their four sons with virtually no cooperation from Jim, Patsy wondered at least once a day, "Was that my baby girl? Did I kill my baby girl?" After a brief recuperation from the abortion, she had thrown herself headlong into nurse's training, hoping that helping others would alleviate some of her own anguish. Six months later she had dropped out of nursing school to marry Terry, the unborn baby's father. He was the one true love of her life. Less than a year after the wedding he left her for another woman.

What if she had kept the baby? Would he have stayed with her? What if she had gone ahead with her nurse's training? Would she have had a better life than the one she struggled with today? True, none of her friends appeared to be any more happily married than she was. But she knew that she could never love Jim the way she had loved Terry.

Patsy's life was a patchwork of regrets. She wished her entire past could be erased. She wanted desperately to start over.

Driving by the Baptist church next door to the doctor's office, a familiar sign caught her eye: "God Is Love."

"I'm *sure*. If He's so full of love why didn't He keep me from ruining my life so totally? I don't *believe* there's a God. I hate Terry for leaving me. And I hate myself for being such a complete and absolute *fool*!"

The past can trip us up with regret and bitterness. It can also trap us with thoughts of the "good old days." Either way, what's done is done, for better or for worse.

When I feel myself looking backward over my shoulder, I try to remember a verse of Scripture that's just the prescription for such a malady.

> *Forgetting* what lies behind and
> *reaching forward* to what lies ahead. I
> *press on* toward the goal for the prize of
> the upward call of God in Christ Jesus
> (Philippians 3:13,14 NASB).

More about the past later. Let's move on to the next culprit in the squelching of contentment.

The Disappointing Present

Muriel sat in her cheerful living room surrounded by a surprisingly large collection of scrapbooks. She smiled dreamily as she studied the old photos. Muriel the cheerleader, blonde-haired and radiant. Muriel the valedictorian, white-robed and grave as she recited her carefully worded speech. Muriel and Bob on their first date—still high school seniors. Bob and Muriel, the beautiful teenage bride and groom, showered with rice, their faces aching with smiles.

Her reverie was abruptly interrupted by a loud outcry originating from the children's rooms. She knew immediately that her "adorable" little boys were pounding on each other again, with anything but adorable expressions on their faces. Muriel paused only a moment, deciding whether to interfere. "Boys!" she shouted, charging toward their battle. "Stop it *right now*! David! What are you *doing*?"

"Brian bit me!" David's tear-filled eyes pleaded for justice. "He always bites me," he concluded tragically.

"You two are *both* going to sit in your rooms for ten minutes without saying another word."

"But, Mom . . ."

"Without saying another word! Then *you* go outside, David. And Brian, *you* stay in here and play."

Once order was restored, Muriel returned to her scrapbooks. Somehow, by now, all the pleasure had vanished. She sighed. Life was such an unsatisfying affair. All she had ever wanted to be was a wife and mother. And yet . . .

Muriel always seemed to have everything—popularity, looks, brains. But somehow, she felt like better days were either behind her or just ahead. She felt as though she were missing something very important.

The children were sweet—but she daydreamed of how much sweeter they would be if they didn't fight and bicker. Her husband, Bob, was faithful and responsible—but she liked to imagine a man a little more sophisticated and . . . well, a little more interesting. Her house was attractive and sunny—but her dream home was high on a hill with a view, a pool, and a rose garden.

"Oh, well," Muriel shrugged as she put her scrapbooks back on the bookshelves and headed for the kitchen to make dinner. "I do my best. And better days will come—I just *know* it!"

Muriel and Bob had given their lives to God and had experienced a Christian "rebirth" the year before their marriage. "Jesus will make everything right," she had told herself at the time.

Muriel's many friends were always a little envious of her. It seemed to everyone around her that maybe she had a little more than her share. She had married her handsome high school sweetheart, the captain of the football team. Today he was a reasonably successful insurance salesman. And their boys? They were the talk of the town: Two perfect Gerber babies had grown into "perfect" little gentlemen ages seven and ten—smart, sweet, and special.

On one hand, Muriel knew very well that she was blessed. On the other hand, she rarely felt like thanking God for her blessings. She felt strangely cheated.

Muriel stared through the kitchen window at the old peach tree in the back garden. *It's like me,* she thought sadly. *All its beautiful petals are gone, and there's nothing but green, hard fruit on its branches.*

Suddenly, unexplicably, Muriel began to weep as if her heart would break. "Lord!" she cried out loud. "Why doesn't anything ever *change* around here? Why don't You make me *happy*?"

Once when I was stewing about a problem with my children, a friend told me, "God is in control. His timing is perfect. And He doesn't make mistakes." Three little statements, simple as a nursery rhyme. Do we really believe them?

Sometimes there's more to dealing with the present than we might imagine at first glance. We'll take a closer look later on. Meanwhile, if today seems bad, what about tomorrow?

The Disenchanting Future

Gina drove as fast as she could toward the house. The kids would be trying to figure out what to feed themselves for dinner by now. Little Miranda was peeking through the curtains when she drove up. A happy smile curved her pretty mouth when she saw the car turn into the driveway. "Mommy's home!" Gina could hear the cheerful announcement as she grabbed the bag of groceries and scurried into the house. "Mom! We're starving! What are you making for dinner?" Jesse eyed the grocery bag hopefully.

"Sorry, kids, but it's tuna casserole again."

A trio of groans answered her.

She looked at the three little faces in front of her. Love surged within her, and tears burned in her eyes momentarily. "Listen—I don't have time to make anything better. I've got to go out again tonight. . . I have a client, and I have to show him a property before dark."

More groans.

"Mom, how come you never stay home anymore?"

"I was home last night, silly." She gently cupped her hand under her only son's chin. "And I've told you before, I have to work a lot of extra hours since Daddy left. It's the only way we're going to have any tuna casserole or anything else to eat around here!"

At the mention of "Daddy," Carmen changed the subject abruptly. "Grandma called a few minutes ago. She said she'd call you back later."

Gina always felt uneasy when she thought about talking to her mother. Five generations of Italian families, and *she* had to be the first one to get a divorce! Since the day Vince left, her mother had been unable to hide her disappointment and humiliation. The Italian mama, informed Gina, "*Sure* day gotta have other women sometimes. But if'a you treat the husband good, he always come'a back to you again."

Apparently Gina hadn't treated Vince "good"— his five-year affair with Lisa had finally ended their marriage. He had left Gina with their son and daughter along with his own daughter from his previous marriage. He and Lisa were now living blissfully in a condominium near the marina.

Gina had always dabbled in real estate. Now she found herself showing properties seven days a week, 12 to 14 hours a day. Soon she would have to take a series of courses in order to get her broker's license. She knew that seeking a larger share of the commissions was the only way she would be able to keep financially afloat.

"Mom, why don't you marry Dominic?" Little Miranda asked innocently. "Then you wouldn't have to work so hard." Dominic was the girls' favorite man—the middle-aged gardener who came once a week to keep the yard looking manicured.

"*Dominic?*" Gina laughed uproariously. Soon her laughter was silenced by her own thoughts about men and marriage. She had loved Vince with all her heart. He had left his first wife for her, so she had been sure he loved her.

Gina had never dreamed that being a single parent would prove to be as difficult as the last nine months had been. But marry again? Worse yet, love again?

"I'll probably never get married again, Miranda. So don't get any ideas about Dominic or anybody else."

The conversation had made her stomach churn. She opened the tuna can and absently drained it into the sink. Financial pressure was her constant companion. She was forever conscious of the tall stack of unpaid bills growing daily on her desk.

At the same time, terrors about leaving the children at home alone in the afternoons haunted her. What would she do when summer came?

She had once thought she was happy, and her happiness had exploded into a shattering divorce. Would she ever feel happiness again? The children gave her pleasure, but she was experiencing so much guilt for not spending time with them that even they could barely cheer her with their familiar, loving faces.

What did the future hold for them?

Nervously she served the meager meal. She had intended to eat with the kids, but all at once she couldn't face the food.

"Mom! You're not eating again?"

"It's okay. I've got to get ready to go. There's ice cream for dessert."

"Mom. . .come on. Eat with us."

"I'm not hungry, baby."

The future *can* be enough to ruin anybody's

appetite. These days some pretty terrifying possibilities lurk around the corner.

Have you ever noticed that in the Bible's lengthiest portion about women, Proverbs 31, the "virtuous" woman is described as one who "smiles at the future"? That gives me hope!

It's fairly easy to see that our three Cinderellas have "fairytale tower" escapes in store. We'll finish their stories later! Meanwhile, let's take a look at *us*—you and me.

Perhaps a good starting point in diagnosing our own "Cinderella Syndrome" is with two important questions: *What is it I am really longing for? How does what I want line up with what God wants for me?*

In reality, God is the One who can coordinate and provide for us the people, places, and things that can make our lives fulfilling. But is He the One we are looking to for help? As we'll discover later, sometimes we focus our eyes on other human beings, expecting them to "make it happen." Looking for a "fairy godmother" is certainly a symptom of the Cinderella Syndrome. And it may be as simple as the process of searching for a better doctor, a more clever attorney, a top-notch realtor, or a best friend. It could be the dream of a new baby. And, of course, it can always be the quest for a perfect (or more perfect) husband.

Unfortunately, the last of the big-time fairy godmothers vanished with the passing of Walt Disney. Are you still watching for yours? There is Someone who can change everything for us.

But He demands that we have no other gods before Him. And He wants us to allow Him to have authority in every part of our lives.

All too often we Christians claim that we really, *really* want God's will in our lives. Yet when we are forced to take our deep desires to Him for approval, we hesitate to do it.

Suppose I want the love of a man who is somebody else's husband? Suppose I want a bigger house just to show my sister that my husband is more successful than hers? Suppose I want something evil to happen to someone who has wronged me?

If I genuinely call myself a "disciple of Jesus" and yet continue to seek after things that fall short of God's will, I am destined to live in frustration and discontent. In fact, if I set about to *have my way* no matter what, I may seriously jeopardize my relationship with God. Why? Because I have become an *idolater*.

What picture do you conjure up in your mind when you hear the word "idolatry"? A scantily clad savage bowing down before a bronzed monkey? Yes, that's one example. But there are quite a number of Cinderella-hopefuls who are also worshiping false gods. Colossians 3:5 warns us that we should "put to death . . . covetousness, which is idolatry" (NKJV).

In other words, our covetous attitude (that envious, grasping desire which we cultivate with our fantasy thinking) is tantamount to idolatry. All of our attention is becoming focused on fulfilling this dream (or in getting this person) which we long for. And what about God? He is reduced to dwelling in the shadows of our new idol.

But all longings aren't bad longings. Sometimes God gives us the desires of our hearts—that is, He puts the idea in our minds Himself. Maybe it's a larger home for a cramped family. A little extra money to smooth out the rough places in the monthly budget. A better car. A less-tension-packed job.

We're glad to agree with the theology from Psalm 37:4, that God *will* give us the desires of our hearts. "But *when*?" we demand in our impatience.

Being at peace with God's timing comes with practice. "Yes," "No," and "Wait" are three possible answers to prayer. To most seasoned veterans, "Wait!" is by far the most familiar response. Have you learned to wait and to "delight yourself in the Lord" (verse 4) while you do it?

I don't always bat in that league myself, but I'm practicing.

Of course there are always gray areas. Wishes and wants may be categorized in the "I-don't-know-if-God-wants-this-for-me-or-not" department. Worse yet, we may not even know what *we* want. In such cases, we can refer to the book of James and its wonderful advice on decision-making:

> If any of you lacks wisdom, let him ask of God, who gives to all men liberally and without reproach, and it will be given to him (James 1:5 NKJV).

For the believer, one thing remains sure: God is the Lord of the past, of the present, and of the future. He can forgive, transform, and fulfill with the touch of His hand. Because of Him, no time of our lives need be disillusioning, disappointing, or disenchanting.

In light of this, let's take one more look at the Cinderella Syndrome itself. This "malady" has been recognized and addressed by more than one feminist author. The best-known of all their books is *The Cinderella Complex* by Colette Dowling. She says:

> We have only one real shot at "liberation" and that is to emancipate ourselves from within. It is the thesis of this book that personal, psychological dependency—the deep wish to be taken care of by others—is the chief force holding women down today. I call this "The Cinderella Complex"—a network of largely repressed attitudes and fears that keeps women in a kind of half-light, retreating from the full use of their minds and creativity. Like Cinderella, women today are still waiting for something external to transform their lives.

Because we are Christian believers, we know that "within" us there is no real answer. Any prideful "shot at liberation" can only lead to the even greater bondage of emptiness and futility. Humanism's arrogant answers are forever hollow, for they leave out the Way, the Truth, and the Life.

Yet the fact remains that there *is* an epidemic of Cinderellas. And Christian women are anything but vaccinated. As a matter of fact, some of us are the worst offenders because we *spiritualize* the fairy tale.

In the hard light of day, and in all honesty, just what are the "external somethings" we are anxiously awaiting? Are our mythical saviors really on their way? Who said so? And are they really worth waiting for?

Chapter Four

Mything Out On Life

Stacy blended the eye shadow carefully across her upper lid. She was a real artist when it came to putting on her face. *Sapphire blue to match the color of my eyes*, she thought as she reached for her mascara.

Dab. Rub. Smooth. Powder. Stacy worked for a full 15 minutes before she was satisfied. Inside her a familiar flutter came and went as she thought about a young man at work. *John will be there today. I've got to look my best!* She reached for a lavender blouse and matched it to a blue-and-purple skirt. After a lavish spritzing with Shalimar, she grabbed her handbag and rushed out the door.

I'm late, Stacy sighed. *But looking good is more important.*

When she arrived at the office, no one seemed to notice the extra pains she had taken with herself. Even John, who had given her polite attention in recent weeks, seemed lost in his business affairs.

Stacy was surprisingly unruffled. She was used to this sort of thing. She nursed an average of three crushes every six months. And each one of them temporarily gave her a new reason to live. *Eventually*, she promised herself, *Mr. Right is going to come along.*

Not an unattractive young woman, Stacy was the type that scared men away with her overwhelming desire to please. Her whole life was obsessively wrapped up in "the man" of the moment. Whether she dated or merely dreamed, she was in love with love. And so far, there were no takers in the marriage market.

Was Snow White a snow job? Snow White sang, "Someday My Prince Will Come." And in all her Disney-girl sincerity she convinced thousands of women that a soon-to-arrive man would bring them happiness and fulfillment.

This idea of a woman waiting for her Prince to rescue her is a classic case of fantasy thinking.

For many girls marriage does begin a time of great fulfillment. It promises children, stability, and an end to the singles scene. But marriage is usually not quite what the fairy tale promised. Why? Because in fantasyland the book closes when the vows are said. The story always ends at the altar.

In the real world a happy, contented wife was once a happy, contented single woman. She is a woman who learned long ago to extract satisfaction from her present circumstances, no matter what her marital status.

When my own daughters started dating, they had a lot of questions about how they would recognize "Mr. Right."

"Maybe there *is* no Mr. Right," Hal told them over dinner one night. "There may be several men you *could* fall in love with and marry."

Pam frowned. "But it's important that I don't miss the right one."

"The important thing for you girls to do is not to *wait* for this man to appear on the scene. Just prepare your lives and hearts so you'll be ready when and if he shows up. Marriage is not a goal. It's a happening."

Singles need to take charge of their relationships with the opposite sex. Are you in a relationship with a "Prince Charming" which you secretly know cannot be the will of God for you? Then, as the Bible says, "If your right hand offends you, cut it off." Let's face it—is it easier to cut off a dog's tail one inch at a time, or all at once? Initially the pain may be greater, but the healing process will come more quickly when we in obedience refuse to permit what God will not allow.

"Someday My Prince Will Come . . ."

Probably the most devastating myth of the

entire Cinderella Syndrome is the "Someday My Prince Will Come" dream. And it doesn't always stop with the last peal of the wedding bells.

Norma is a lovely, vivacious gal with a solid marriage. One sunny afternoon she asked me over for coffee. We sat on her shadow-dappled patio next to the sparkling pool. Our conversation took a surprising turn.

"Somehow I'm dissatisfied, Lee."

"With what, Norma? What's the problem?"

"Oh, I don't know. Just life in general, I guess. And Harry really can be a bore at times. I guess things just seem like they should be more exciting than they are. Especially Harry."

I was puzzled by this unexpected revelation until we wandered through her spacious house on my way out. Then, on her carefully dusted bookshelf, I noticed a vast and colorful array of gothic-style romance novels. I had always known she enjoyed reading, but I didn't know what she read.

"So you're into harlequin romances! I'll bet you watch the soaps too, don't you?" I asked the question with the biggest smile I could muster.

Norma flushed a bit. "Well, I'll have to admit I'm hooked on two or three of them."

"You know, that just may be a big part of your problem. Poor Harry! How do you expect him to match up with those hunks in your book and on TV?"

Norma chuckled a little. "Well I'm not sure that's really the problem, but you could have a point. What are you suggesting?"

"Really want to know? I suggest that you go

cold turkey for 30 days. No romanticizing. No syrupy novels. No soap operas!" She grimaced, but finally agreed.

What a thrill it was to have her call me a month later!

"I never would have *believed* that my thought life and my real life were so tangled up! I was actually more involved in fantasy than in reality. No wonder I was so discontented! I was concentrating on everyone else's hot romances and neglecting to cultivate my own!"

"Great! But what about poor old boring Harry?"

"Oh, Lee . . ." she laughed happily. "Harry's not so boring after all. We've started over again. And I've promised him no more TV competition."

Any woman who lives in an imaginary world causes her reality to suffer. This is often why the prince never arrives. He's usually just a figment of the imagination anyway!

Looking for external solutions to inner dissatisfaction doesn't stop with "Someday my prince will come." Granted, that's the most familiar form it takes. But some women subscribe to the myth that their dissatisfaction is all wrapped up in the behavior of other people.

"Someday My People Will Change . . ."

"If only my teenagers would shape up . . ."

"If only my husband were a *real* Christian . . ."

"If only my circle of friends was a bit more intellectual . . ."

The hope of people changing can be particularly troublesome for Christian women, because it gets confused with a genuine concern and prayer.

Kay is a 67-year-old mother of three. Two of her kids, for one reason or another, have rejected Kay's Christian beliefs. She is a faithful, sincere saint. But she has a continuous gnawing at the pit of her stomach. "I can't *rest* until they are born again," she told me with tears in her eyes.

She fasts. She underlines promises in her Bible. She calls up friends to pray around the clock. And, of course, all of these things are good.

But Kay is also inclined to manipulate. She uses her grandchildren to relay messages to her unbelieving offspring, teaching them Bible verses to recite "for Mommy and Daddy." She gives books from the Christian bookstore for birthdays. And she writes a lot of Scripture-packed letters.

Kay has a couple of serious problems. First of all, she *refuses* to accept peace of mind. "If I stop worrying about them, I'll stop praying for them. And if I stop praying, they'll never change."

The second problem is that Kay is forever communicating her disapproval to her children. She does this subtly, but it comes through. "I don't say a word to them," she confided with a wink, "but they get the message!"

Kay's world is a kaleidoscope of dissatisfaction. She is totally preoccupied with getting through to the people she's trying to change. Everything else is second priority.

No doubt most of our concerns for other

people are well-intentioned. When Hal and I were married, I saw a lot of diamond-in-the-rough raw material in him. When he walked me to the altar, I thought, *I'll alter him!*" And if anyone could have changed another person through advice, hounding, cajoling, or any other available form of manipulation, I would have been the champion.

I waged war on Hal's faults for years. But in the crumbs of defeat he turned out to be a tough cookie! I learned that I had to accept him "as is." I decided to continue to love him even if *not one fault was ever changed!* (Sigh!)

This subject offers good news and bad news. The bad news is that nowhere in the Bible did God commission us to change the behavior of another human being. This wouldn't fit into God's plan for man to have free choice and a free will. So He absolutely failed to give us any instruction for remakes of family members or friends. Get the picture?

But the good news is that we don't have to feel like "victims" just hanging on until our people shape up. We can, in God, find contentment *in spite of them*!

"*Someday My* Prosperity *Will Arrive. . . .*"

Another myth that bewitches many a dreamy-eyed Ms. is the midas touch—the wish for wealth or prosperity. Fairytale thinkers often think they simply need a new castle tower (or at least a remodeled one!) to make them happy. They're looking for a new, materialistic horizon. The old one just won't do.

Susan left her husband, determined to make it on her own. He was admittedly a flake, and she had tolerated his inability to provide for her and the children for 22 years. But now at last the kids were gone.

"I'm going to make 50,000 a year," she told me with a strange hardness in her eyes. "I'm going to buy a condo. Get a decent car. Have gorgeous porcelain nails. And my wardrobe is going to be just the way *I* want it."

She set about to accomplish her goals. She attended self-help seminar after success seminar. She learned to turn off her clouded emotions. To use her mind as a tool for accomplishment. To focus on achievement and shut out everything else.

"I don't care if I ever go out with another man. I've had enough emotion and sex to last me three lifetimes. All I want is to live a comfortable life with everything I need at my fingertips."

Within two years Susan was *very* successful. She had her "agenda for the month" taped to her refrigerator. And she never missed a deadline. By the end of year number two she was pushing 60,000 a year, driving a BMW, and dressing in Anne Klein.

"Hey—you've really made it, gal! And in such a short time! How do you feel about things now, Sue?" I asked her one afternoon over a quick cup of tea. We were in a crowded shopping mall. She had business there, and had let me know that her time was very limited. Her eyes darted about, scanning the bustling shoppers. She paused before she answered.

"I don't know, Lee. To tell you the truth, I don't feel much of anything now. I just function. I enjoy not having to worry about money. But now I find myself worrying about other things instead. It's strange. I'm kind of empty inside."

It can be established a thousand times over—*externals simply don't satisfy our inner discontentments*. Temporarily, we may enjoy a sense of accomplishment, relief, or pleasure. But it doesn't last.

Humanist books, like *The Cinderella Complex,* make the point again and again—all satisfaction must come from the Self:

> I have learned that freedom and independence can't be wrested from others —from the society at large, or from men —but can only be developed painstakingly from within. To achieve it we will have to give up the dependencies we've used, like crutches, to feel safe (p. 230).

To some degree this is true. Depression quickly clouds our view when we are depending on outside stimuli.

"I'm stuck in this dumb job."

"My mother doesn't understand me."

"My husband is a loser."

"The kids are always getting into trouble at school."

And no doubt a humanist would consider the

acceptance of Jesus Christ into a life as yet
another "external" crutch, just like looking for
a prince or a fairy godmother.

Nevertheless, we Christians have learned that
without God we aren't whole. Ephesians 2:1-7
shows us that outside of Him we aren't even alive!
And in our new life and wholeness in Him we find
the real, solid answer to the Cinderella Syndrome.

When I was a young girl, subway-hopping beneath the streets of Philadelphia to elude my
dreary home life, I was independent and self-
sufficient, but I had a deep sense of *aloneness*.
And I was often afraid. After I accepted Christ into
my life, I had an "inner" companion. Jesus was
with me everywhere from that moment on. My
troubles didn't magically disappear (as a matter
of fact they got a whole lot worse for a while!),
but God and I were able to face anything together. And with a sense of joy I handled some
unbelievably difficult circumstances.

Without Him we can do nothing. And yet Paul
said, "I can do all things through Christ who
strengthens me" (Philippians 4:13 NKJV).

So which myth is the villain? What is the object of our "myth-directed" thinking? It may be
the Prince, problem people, or personal prosperity that taunts and teases us.

But the real conclusion to any quest for external satisfaction lies in the simple matter of
trusting God.

When I asked Stacy, the falling-in-love-with-
love kid, whether she could trust God to provide

her with the "right" man or to make her content to be single, she made a face, wrinkling her powdered nose.

"Well, sure I believe in God and heaven and all that. But I don't *want* to ask Him to give me what *He* wants. He'll line me up with some spiritual giant who sits around and prays and never wants to have fun. Either that or He'll make me an old maid and send me someplace as a missionary."

When I asked Kay if she could trust God with her non-Christian children, she frowned. "Look, Lee. God helps those who help themselves. My kids are *my* responsibility. If they aren't converted by the time I get to heaven, I'll be guilty before God for their loss!"

And when I asked Susan if she wouldn't want to invite Christ into her life to fill the emotional and spiritual vacuum there, she just smiled. "Thanks, but I don't need a crutch. I'm doing just fine alone. I respect *your* need for a God, Lee. But frankly I think I'd rather handle my life myself than to trust some cosmic force."

Why don't people trust God with their lives? Because they don't realize how much He loves them! A beautiful Psalm tells us:

O Lord, Thou hast searched me and
   known me.
Thou dost know when I sit down and
   when I rise up;
Thou dost understand my thoughts
   from afar.

> Thou dost scrutinize my path and my
>   lying down,
> And art intimately acquainted with all
>   my ways. . . .
> For thou didst form my inward parts;
> Thou didst weave me in my mother's
>   womb. . . .
> In Thy book they were all written,
> The days that were ordained for me,
> When as yet there was not one of them
>   (Psalm 139:1-3,13,16 NASB).

Perhaps the most touching portion of this Psalm says:

> How precious also are Thy thoughts to
>   me, O God!
> How vast is the sum of them!
> If I should count them, they would
>   outnumber the sand (Psalm 139:17,
>   18 NASB).

This is the same God who placed the universe in order and implanted deep emotions in the soul of man and woman. Can He handle our need for love?

This is the same God who set the boundaries of the oceans and designed the magnificent, unique structure of every snowflake. Can He take care of our kids?

This is the same God who feeds the sparrows and who hid treasures of gold, silver, and precious stones in the heart of the earth. Can He cope with our needs for financial security?

Can God really satisfy the longings of our hearts? Can He deal with our dreams? Can He concern Himself with the wild hopes we hide so carefully in our silent thoughts?

The answer obviously is *yes*. But a bigger question remains. Are we willing to let Him do things His way? Can we bring ourselves to cast our cares upon Him and leave them there? Can we really count on Him to make the best of the future and to give us what we need for the present?

Can we learn to believe that the past, with all its intricately woven triumphs and tragedies, belongs to Him now, and that He *really is able* to work all those tangled threads into the picture for good? Let's take a brief look over our shoulders. You may be talking about the "good old days." I may be saying, "Whew! Glad to be out of there!" But some of us may have some unfinished business behind us. Let's find out.

Chapter Five

The Past—
Once Upon A Time

Do you remember Patsy? I introduced you to her just a few pages ago. Patsy was filled with bitterness. She had chosen to have an abortion. She had been rejected by her "true love." She had dropped out of nurse's training. She had married a man whom she always considered to be "second best." And now she blames God, herself, and her family for her desperate hopelessness.

Before we go on, let me tell you about another woman with a problem past. Cheire is a vivacious 33-year-old. Long ago she and her mismatched husband parted company. Their separation climaxed a series of unpleasant circumstances. First Stan had quit his job. Then he had squandered Cheire's savings and had taken up with a former friend's wife. Yet recently Cheire confided in me that her ex-husband Stan was "one of the most sensitive men I ever met." (I wanted to take her temperature. I thought she was delirious!)

Like Patsy, Cheire also tortured herself with the mistakes of her unalterable past. "If only I weren't divorced, I think I would feel better about myself."

One morning after listening to an hour of tearful mourning, I confronted her. "Look, Cheire, the fact is you *are* divorced! Sure, you were the unwilling party in the situation. But how much longer are you going to let this stand between you and happiness? Between you and God?"

Cheire finally broke free of her fairy tale. Yes, she had to face up to Bill's faults and errors. No, she couldn't hold a grudge against him for all the misery he had caused her. She realized that either glorifying or horrifying the past would prevent her from experiencing true happiness today.

Meanwhile, our friend Patsy is still locked in shackles of regret. Although she blames herself for making some bad choices, she is inclined to turn her frustration toward her husband and kids. And of course, God let it all happen. So to her He is the guiltiest party of all.

Patsy isn't the first woman to blame her unhappiness on someone else. There was another homemaker who lived on Eden Street in The Garden City, many years ago. While Eve was eating of the forbidden fruit, God caught her redhanded. The story, in Genesis chapter 3, records her great creativity at self-justification. Eve immediately blamed her own disobedience and unhappiness on outside pressures! Naturally her husband, Adam, was implicated. And she was the absolute first in history to say, "The devil made me do it!"

I don't know about you, but every time something goes wrong in *my* house, everyone's first reaction is, "Okay, who's to blame?" Even Jesus encountered this same thinking in John. When the local busybodies met up with the blind man, they piously inquired of the Lord, "Okay, who sinned? This man or his parents? *Why* was he born blind?" They assumed someone else was to blame.

Who is it that *we* blame for past sorrows? An unloving mother? A physically abusive father? An insensitive grammar school teacher who whacked our hands in front of the whole class? An older brother or sister who ridiculed us constantly? Or (heaven forbid!) God?

Not many Christians openly admit their anger with God. They don't even recognize that they are blaming Him for the disappointing and traumatic past. And if we secretly harbor anger against God, it's just not possible to rejoice in "*this* day which the Lord has made." We're still hung up about the day He made "yesterday"!

Author and Christian counselor John Powell writes: (*Why Am I Afraid to Love*, Argus Communications Co., 1967)

When you repress or suppress those

things which you don't want to live with, you don't really solve the problem, because you don't bury the problem dead, you bury it alive. It will remain alive and active until it is dealt with.

Unlike our science-fiction heroes, we will never be permitted to enter into a "time warp." We can't go backward and change events. But we *can* do something about the *effect* the past is having on the present.

Sometimes our regrets are due to bad decisions. We suspect that we've taken the wrong turn at the fork in the road.

"I should *never* have given up my
    scholarship to get married."
"If only I had taken that job in Seattle."
"Why on earth did I buy this horrible car?"

Perhaps a different decision *would* have been more satisfying. But the pointlessness of regret is this: There is one thing that even God can't change—the past. On the other hand, He is the one Person who can heal us from its crippling effects.

EMPTINESS is the by-product
of the search for happiness.

HAPPINESS is the by-product
of the search for meaning.

Bad decisions aren't the only things that contribute to our sense of sorrow. Most circumstances are not chosen—they just happen. We didn't select our parents, our sex, or our heritage. We didn't pick out our talents (or lack of them!). We've had little or no control over many of the events that punctuate our personal stories. In fact if we had been the author, we probably would have edited out a few chapters!

Along with our inability to direct the flow of our own history comes the temptation to use the past as an excuse. And there's *always* an excuse available.

"I can't help it. . . I was the middle child, and you know what *that* means!"

"What do you expect? I was the youngest in the family!"

"Hey! I'm the oldest child in the family. Everyone has *always* expected too much from me."

"Well, really, being an only child is a lot of the reason I'm the way I am."

The past can certainly *explain* our behavior. But never should we attempt to *excuse* ourselves by clinging to musty old memories.

My youngest daughter got away with all kinds of things as a child. She escaped indictments for bad grades, bad moods, and bad incidents. Why? Because everyone forgave her behavior with "Well, poor little thing. . . she's lost *two* mothers." Today as a mature young woman, she admits that she frequently used her past to excuse her present. Now she has elected to be a healthy, whole person in spite of the tragedies of her childhood.

And as for me, I'm also trying to resist living in the past, to stop complaining about things that are already over and done.

I am trying to drop phrases like:

> You should have. . .
> How come you didn't. . .
> If you had stopped for gas back there. . .
> Why didn't you. . .

I am also trying to stop saying:

> I should have. . .
> How come I didn't. . .
> If I had stopped for gas back there. . .
> Maybe I should have written this book
>   three years ago. . .

My job is to live, carving out contentment, NOW—not *to live* in the past, but simply *to learn* from the past.

Does time really heal all wounds? Not necessarily. The mending of memories requires more than the passing of years. Often pain from the past can jump back out at us as if it had just occurred.

Shakespeare warned us that we all "suffer the slings and arrows of outrageous fortune." How unfair it would be if God should allow victims to suffer all their lives because of the evil actions of others! How unjust it would be if God left us disabled by the past, powerless against its effects on our present! But He doesn't! He has provided some solid principles for starting over.

Here's one simple fact:

> *They* are responsible for the *past*;
> *You* are responsible for the *present*.

That's good news! If your father mistreated you in the past, your father is responsible for his actions. If your husband was unfaithful, your husband is guilty of that indiscretion. If you've been offended by a friend, your friend is accountable for that unkindness.

Sometimes when I have a flashback of some unresolved past situation, I try to convince myself that it's "just a passing thought. By the end of the day it won't bother me anymore." But I've learned that unresolved issues will continue to come back to haunt me again and again until I make the effort to deal with them once and for all.

God gave us some great advice in Ephesians 4:26: "Don't let the sun go down on your wrath." Certainly Jesus wasn't naive enough to believe that every one of our problems could be fully solved before 8 P.M. But He did advise us to *deal* with our negative emotions before then.

The question is *how have we responded*?

Getting Forgiveness

Before we get down to the business of for-

giving, let's *be forgiven*. "For what? I was an in-
nocent victim!" Cheire's eyes flashed when I sug-
gested that she needed forgiveness herself. "After
what I've been through? What are you talking
about?"

We need forgiveness for *attitudes* as well as for
actions. Perhaps we've been bitter or resentful.
You may be harboring an "I'll get even" vow. I
may be withholding my love in an icy, hostile
way. None of these surly stances is pleasing to
our Lord.

But what a wonderful promise God records for
us in 1 John 1:9: "If we confess our sins, He is
faithful and just to forgive us our sins and to
cleanse us from all unrighteousness" (NKJV).
Why don't you receive your forgiveness now? But
let's mean what we say: ". . . and forgive us our
trespasses, *as we forgive those who trespass
against us.* Once we've done this, we can move
on to the next step. After *getting* forgiveness, we
need to *give forgiveness.*

Giving Forgiveness: To God

God, who never sleeps, concerns Himself with
the welfare of even the dumbest, dustiest sparrows. He was not "out to lunch" when that painful event occurred. He was aware of the agony
that ensued. He allowed it to happen. He did not
interfere.

Now we know that God makes no mistakes.
But have you been angry (or secretly resentful)
at God for not intervening on your behalf? For

allowing hurt to cross your path? I have. And I've learned that, presumptuous as it sounds, we must "forgive" God. We must tell Him—out loud—that we won't hold anger and resentment toward Him any longer. We need to honestly trust and accept His decision to permit pain to enter our lives. Will you allow Him to beautifully weave tragedy, like dark threads, into your life's tapestry?

Just take a moment and tell Him, "Father, I'm sorry I've been angry at You. I want You to know I accept Your decisions for my life. Your will be done!" When you forgive God, you free His hands to massage your hurts and to repair your damaged spirit. My husband, Hal, recalls the day he voiced his forgiveness toward God for not intervening in the deaths of his wives. Only after that did Hal begin to sense the healing of his wounds. When he tells the story today, he says, "It's as if it happened to another man. The memory isn't gone, but the hurt has really been healed!"

Whether we're forgiving God or just another mortal, forgiving is forgetting. We don't forget the circumstances; it's the painful emotions that we're unable to recapture. Or look at it this way: If you can still feel the hurt or the anger, you haven't really forgiven the one who caused it! And that may include *you*!

Giving Forgiveness: To Yourself

As we saw before, we've all made bad decisions. Can you forgive yourself for your mistakes, for your poor choices, for "letting the fish get away"? Can you forgive yourself for the sins you willfully and knowingly committed? God is willing to forgive you for *anything*. Shouldn't you be just as generous? More specifically, if we don't accept God's forgiveness, we are usurping His lordship!

"Repent" is almost a buzzword in some Christian circles. "Sinners, repent!" makes me think of hellfire and brimstone. But to repent actually means *to change direction*. An old hymn defines repent in its title: "Turn Back, Oh Man." To repent is to turn back toward God. And once you've repented, you are forgiven, That's all there is to it!

So . . . off the couch. Into the bathroom. Look deeply into the mirror and repeat after me:

> "_____, God has forgiven you for your foolish mistakes as well as your intentional sins. It's all over. Finished.
>
> "I accept God's free gift of forgiveness. I joyfully apply it to my special circumstances. I therefore have no choice but to forgive myself!"

Giving Forgiveness: To Others

Are you ready? Now is the time for our final forgiveness phase. "Why should I forgive someone who doesn't *deserve* forgiveness?" Patsy asked me bitterly one day. Worse yet, the "transgressor" may not even be asking for forgiveness. He may never have said, "I'm sorry."

Jesus, as He hung on the cross, looked down at the people who put Him there, and cried, "Father, forgive them, for they know not what they do." Like those angry, murderous crowds, we don't deserve God's mercy. But He freely forgives us. And in turn He expects us to show mercy toward each other. We will *be* forgiven of our own trespasses (as we say in The Lord's Prayer) ". . . *as we forgive those* who trespass against us."

"It's impossible," you might reply, "I *can't* forgive (_____). You just don't know what horrible things he/she has done to me." We may still be burning with rage. Yet God says we *must* forgive. But how?

Forgiveness doesn't *start* with an overwhelming sense of love and compassion; it *ends* with that. Initially, forgiveness is a *decision* plus two words: "I forgive." Making the decision, then saying the words, breaks the dam. Rivers of love and compassion are then set free to surge through our hearts.

Now. . . set the book aside again for a moment. Grab a pad of paper and a pencil. Can you think of someone or some experience that still causes you pain? Can you still feel anger or hurt over some particular incident? Close your eyes and let your mind scan the pages of your past. If an unpleasant or still-stinging memory pops up, jot down that circumstance or that person's name.

As you prayerfully review your list of unresolved hurts, remember to forgive God for per-

mitting these events to happen. Seek His forgiveness for any mistakes or trespasses on your part.
Then, speaking their names out loud, address the
perpetrators. Give them the benefit of the doubt.
Perhaps they weren't aware of the pain they
caused, or weren't conscious of the long-range
effects their acts would have on you. ("They know
not what they do.") Leave them in God's hands
to show them the error of their ways.

If the person is still living, and knows about the
problem, you might feel better if you tell him that
you've forgiven him. Perhaps the relationship can
be restored.

But what if that person you're forgiving today
has already died? Unforgiveness toward someone
who is dead is an almost impossible burden to
bear. We mull over the things we wished we had
said or done while there was still time. It is important for us to speak out our forgiveness toward the late reprobate! In doing so we transfer
all the emotional baggage off our shoulders onto
God's.

Because of his battle with alcoholism, my
father inflicted hurts on every member of our
family. He was often abusive when drunk. And,
as many alcoholics do, he deteriorated mentally
and physically as each year went by. Once I became a Christian, I wanted to share my experience in Christ with Dad, but I never felt I could
get through to him.

After my mother, sisters, and I left him in Philadelphia and moved to California, I wrote him a
long letter. I told him all about my relationship

with Jesus. And I added that, as a result of this, I was able to forgive him for all the times he had hurt me. Father never answered the letter, though I know he received it. He died shortly thereafter of cirrhosis of the liver.

I have no idea if my letter caused my father to reevaluate his life. I don't know if it drew him closer to God. But I fulfilled my obligation to forgive, and today I'm so thankful that I followed God's instruction in time. Do you have a few letters to write? A few phone calls to make? Follow God's directions. Don't let another sun set before you've cleared the unforgiveness from your heart.

Forgiveness is the place where we *begin* to restore love. I like what Karen Burton Mains says about the benefits of forgiveness in her book *The Key to a Loving Heart*:

> The results of forgiveness are well worth the struggle of yanking our wills to the painful point of obedience. Finding the possible in the impossible is always a thrill! It jolts our stodgy humanity.

But forgiveness, the cure for past pain, is like most medication: *We* have to fill the prescription. *We* have to take the pills.

Patsy chose to continue in her disillusionment and despair. She continues to blame everyone, including God and herself, for the blighted years behind her. And she's still a very unhappy woman.

Cheire decided to take our four past-mending

steps. She accepted God's forgiveness for her bad attitudes and actions. She forgave God for allowing the hurt to enter her life. She forgave herself, appropriating God's grace in her own life. She forgave Stan, while acknowledging his weakness and failures. Today she has begun to live a contented, fulfilled life.

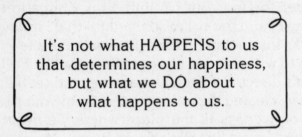

It's not what HAPPENS to us
that determines our happiness,
but what we DO about
what happens to us.

Beyond forgiveness, there is one more wonderful fact that can't be overlooked. In God's Word there is a simple statement found in Romans 8:28. If it isn't already underlined in your Bible, it should be!

> We know that all things work together
> for good to those who love God, to those
> who are the called according to His pur-
> pose (NKJV).

In this sparkling jewel of a promise lies the joyful resolution of the past.

In "all things" lies the hope of a happy future.

And in this spectacular pledge from the Creator God to us, we find a vast treasure for *today*. Because of Him, contentment is available *right now*. Because of His authority, there can be no fear, no anxiety, no gnawing doubt.

In His overwhelming love, we discover peace with the past. Peace for the future. Peace in the present hour.

Chapter Six

The Present—
The Barefoot Cinderella

You remember Muriel. She was the ex-cheer-leader who entered our lives in Chapter 3. If you recall, Muriel wasn't quite satisfied with life in the present day. And it wasn't regret that held her back, either. Her past was relatively trauma-free.

One of Muriel's hang-ups was her preoccupation with the "good old days." She was still enjoying the crisp cold nights when high school football games filled the autumn air with cheers and songs. She was still reliving sun-baked summer days when rows of oil-coated friends tanned side-by-side along a surf-washed beach. Still trying to recapture bustling, busy days of classes and cliques, of dreams and dates. If only she could go back there again!

And other "if onlys" taunted Muriel too. Her home wasn't her dream house. Her kids weren't perfect. Her husband? Well. . . .

I like what author David Wilkerson once said:

> I wish every homemaker could hear me say, "Step out of your bondage of living your life only through others!" God never intended that you find happiness only through your husband or your children. I am not suggesting that you forsake them, only that you forsake your degrading bondage to the idea that your happiness depends only on other people. God wants you to discover a life of true happiness and contentment, based only on what you are as a person, and not on the moods and whims of people around you.

People. Places. Things. They all contribute to our unsettled sense of "it could be better," yet the problem nearly always lies internally, not externally.

My friend Sue Ellen got up on Saturday morning feeling tired, cranky, and more than a little dissatisfied. The first thing that caught her eye as she descended the bedroom stairs was her sickly green, tattered living room carpeting.

Yuk! She thought to herself. *If only I had a*

*new carpet. Then this house could begin to look
nice. That stuff is an eyesore. It ruins everything.*

Since Sue Ellen is a Christian, she tries to read
her Bible every day. That particular morning, she
listlessly turned to her daily chapter. It was in Ec-
clesiastes 6. Like a spotlight, verse 9 suddenly
penetrated her gloom.

"What the eye sees is better than what the soul
desires" (NASB).

Sue Ellen turned and looked out the window
at the new day. A gentle breeze stirred the oak
tree branches. Clouds scooted happily across the
bright blue sky.

"Oh, God!" She laughed aloud, "How can I be
such a grouch? Here I have this whole beautiful
day from You and I'm griping about my carpet!
How absurd!"

She shared with me later that afternoon a reali-
zation that had struck her all at once: "If God had
really wanted me to have new carpeting today,
somebody somehow would have showed up
yesterday and recarpeted my house! What I have
right now is *exactly* what God wants me to have!"

The "If Onlys"

Even though most of us grasp this concept in-
tellectually, any one of us could probably sign
the following statement:

> I could be "woman of the year" *if only*
> a few things would change:

1) *My Circumstances*

- If I had more money (or if I didn't have to worry about our investments).
- If I lived in a bigger house (or if I didn't have so many rooms to clean).
- If I had a child (or if I didn't have so many problems with my children).

2) *My Family*

- If my kids were more helpful (or if they would just leave me with an empty nest!)
- If I had a husband (or if my husband weren't around so much).
- If my husband were more thrifty (or if he weren't such a Scrooge).

3) *My Self*

- If I were prettier (or if people didn't like me just for my looks).
- If I could lose this weight (or if I weren't so bony).
- If I didn't have this physical problem (or if I were more spiritual).

Muriel was a classic Cinderella when it came to the present. But she eventually recovered from her troubles. Unfortunately, it took a near-tragedy to open her eyes.

One rainy afternoon her eldest son, David, rushed out in front of a car. Muriel never knew what he was chasing. She heard the screeching of brakes. She ran outside in time to see his broken little body lying in the street.

"Jesus!" she screamed. "Don't let my baby die!" The ambulance ride to the emergency room was a time of terror like nothing she had ever known before.

For two exhausting weeks she waited beside his hospital bed. He clung to life, but for days no one could safely say that he would ever awaken from his coma.

Muriel's husband, Bob, his eyes red from weeping and lack of sleep, stayed faithfully at her side. He prayed with her, and together they agonizingly gave their firstborn boy back to God. "He's Yours," Bob sobbed. "Your will be done."

Little brother Brian was shuffled from Grandma to Aunt, from friend to friend. When she could, Muriel held him tightly in her arms. How precious his tiny life had become! As she watched him crawl into bed one night she thought, *He's alive. Healthy. Normal. What a beautiful gift he is*!

Early the fifteenth morning, once again Muriel quietly tiptoed into David's hospital room. Unexpectedly he turned his head, looked directly at her, and smiled. "David!" she whispered. "Do you know who I am?"

"Mommy . . ." he answered thickly. "You're Mommy."

Muriel fell on her knees, thanking God for the miracle. Two weeks later David was home, making an amazing recovery.

Throughout this traumatic time, Muriel began to grasp how very precious "normal" life is. She began to see that she had taken for granted many of God's good and perfect gifts.

"Lee, why do we overlook so many blessings? I'm ashamed of the way I thought for so long. I was so ungrateful."

"I don't know, Muriel. But I've done the same thing myself. A friend of mine has an interesting statement written in the front of her Bible: "We never fully love anything until we realize it might be lost."

"That's sure been true for me!" Muriel's eyes blurred with tears.

Do we, like Muriel, have to be pushed to the wall to develop contentment? A needlepoint sampler I've seen reads:

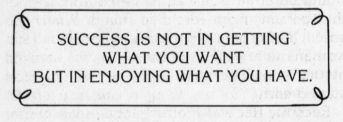

SUCCESS IS NOT IN GETTING
WHAT YOU WANT
BUT IN ENJOYING WHAT YOU HAVE.

Are "if onlys" standing in the way of our sense of contentment? Besides surrounding circum-stances and conditions, we often blame other people for our present state of mind.

Habit Patterns of Feeling

"He makes me so angry."

"She makes me feel so intimidated!"

"You make me happy."

Did you know that other people do not make us feel a certain way? We create our own feelings, and we do it by habit. I can prove this.

Suppose you and several other people were to arrive late to a meeting with a group of strangers. If everyone were looking at you, what would *your* reaction be? Well, if the strangers in the room were really responsible for producing your feelings, then those feelings would be identical in every latecomer.

You, for example, might say that you were quite self-conscious and embarrassed because the strangers were staring at you. But not everyone would have this reaction. Another woman might feel angry because they had started the meeting without her. A second lady would be afraid she had missed something. A third person might feel thrilled that she had been absent during only half the meeting. And a fourth woman might insist that she had simply arrived at the scheduled time and the meeting had started early!

Recently Hal and I joined another couple for breakfast. We were served by an obnoxious and pushy waiter. The other husband was so disturbed by this waiter's service that he insisted, "He's ruined my meal! He has absolutely spoiled my appetite!"

Yet this was not true. Out of the four of us, he was the only one who had this reaction. It really wasn't the waiter's responsibility (creep that he was). Our friend's breakfast was spoiled by his own habit of reacting in a certain way to certain events.

Sometimes I hang up the phone and say to myself, "She intimidates me!" When this occurs, I have to rethink. The person on the other end of the line *cannot make me feel intimidated* or any other way (although she may be *very* intimidating). The fact is that I have *allowed myself* to be intimidated.

Many times we say, "You make me so angry!" Yet we've been the ones with the angry feelings. We need to learn that we *choose* our emotions.

No longer do we have to live life as a *thermometer*. A thermometer takes the temperature of others and reflects it.

"I wonder what kind of a mood he'll be in today."

"I hope she doesn't make me mad!"

"Am I fitting in okay?"

Instead, let's work at becoming a *thermostat*! That way we won't just take the temperature of others but will set our own "comfort zone"!

"No matter what kind of a mood he's in, I'm going to be cheerful."

"I won't allow myself to be angered by her anymore."

"Today is the day the Lord has made; I will rejoice and be glad in it."

When we predetermine our own attitude before going into a situation, we don't have to say, "I just hope it will be a good day!"

Equally treacherous are statements like:

"I've gained six pounds. . . . the holidays are to blame!"

"My language is bad because of the people I work with."

"I'm depressed. . . I wish it would stop raining so I could cheer up."

"I'll have to cheat on my time sheet because I'm so broke."

As we said before, we are responsible to God for our attitudes and actions. As we lose ourselves in His love, His will, and His plan for our lives, His Spirit fills us. We gain the "fruits" the Bible describes in Galatians chapter 5.

Love
Joy
Peace
Patience
Kindness
Goodness
Faithfulness
Gentleness
Self-control

If you consistently lack any of these qualities, check out your walk with Jesus. Maybe the problem lies there. Maybe it lies in your tendency to depend on other people instead of on Him.

Sometimes, like so many wide-eyed Easter bunnies, we hide our colorful "happiness eggs" in someone else's "basket."

That person invariably doesn't care as much about our happiness as we do. Sometimes he (or she or they) drops the basket. Sometimes he gets lost on the freeway. Sometimes he walks away and leaves us . . . empty-handed.

Just as others can't "make" us feel intimidated or angry, they really can't make us happy either. And we shouldn't expect them to. Yet emotional dependency is a trap into which we can all tumble.

Emotional Dependency

A short time ago I watched an interview with a battered wife. "But *why*?" asked the reporter. "Why did you stay with your husband when he was so abusive?" The battered wife smiled sadly as she replied, "Because I had grown *emotionally dependent upon him*; I couldn't leave him." This kind of emotional dependency of one human being upon another human being should be illegal. It certainly breeds trouble.

For years I depended on my husband to meet my emotional needs. It was a terrible burden on him, and he recoiled under the pressure. How wonderful to know that someone else never holds the key to our emotional stability or happiness!

When we place our faith and trust in the Lord, we can "commit our way unto the Lord, trust also in Him, and He shall bring it to pass" (Psalm 37:5). *He* will bring to pass our emotional stability and tranquility, for He has promised in Isaiah 26:3, "Thou wilt keep him in perfect peace whose mind is stayed on Thee, because he trusts in Thee."

As Christian women we have received many gifts from God. We will have to account to Him if we allow our emotional dependency on a man (or human approval in general) to stand in the way of uncompromised efforts. "Success" in God's eyes means doing our absolute best for His kingdom and His glory. And we should be content in *doing* our best, unconcerned about *being* the best.

Yet the need to "be loved" takes its toll on many of us. It lies behind much fear of honest communication. It explains many of our slavish, obedient responses to unreasonable demands. And it correlates with far more deadly conditions—such as anorexia nervosa.

"Please love me!" women cry out in thought, in word, and in deed. If only God's unconditional, personal love could be understood and taken to heart! Then our unhealthy cravings for people's applause would be lost in His smile. "Well done!" Jesus says in the parable of the talents. "You are good and faithful in the little things. Soon I'll bless you with more!" Isn't that approval enough?

Dependency swings like a pendulum during our lifetimes. At one point I was totally independent of any church; years later I was hopelessly dependent upon my church to make me happy. During another phase I was so emotionally dependent upon my husband that I was handicapped; when the pendulum returned, I didn't really care what he thought. None of these extremes is particularly constructive.

Let's not strive for the kind of *dependence*

that makes us weak and emotionally crippled. But let's also avoid an *independence* that touts, "I am woman; I am invincible." The godly balance, I believe, comes with knowing that *we can be free to enjoy other people without depending upon them.*

Unfortunately, some women have gotten themselves caught in the pendulum swing of resisting male authority. They probably do this because of past disappointments. You find these well-intentioned ladies striving for parity with men, and fighting for their rights.

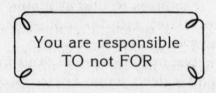

You are responsible
TO not FOR

Do you want to be free to enjoy the present? Take heart! Your life will be flooded with freedom the moment you recognize that you are responsible *to* and not *for* other people.

Take a mother, for example (or mother-in-law!). I'm responsible *to* the Lord to be the daughter He wants me to be. (Remember that a *grown* daughter is different from a *growing* daughter.) I am responsible *to* love Mom, *to* honor her. But I am not responsible *for* her habits, her lifestyle, or her moods.

Consider a husband. He is responsible, before God, *to* be the head of his household, *to* love his wife, *to* be faithful to his wife. But this fellow is *not* responsible *for* his wife's actions, her decisions, or her behavior.

Look at friendship. I am responsible *to* be the kind of friend I am supposed to be. I am responsible *to* keep in touch, *to* care, *to* go the extra mile. I am not responsible *for* my friend's moods. She may telephone me and whine, "You hardly ever call me! I'm so lonely, and I feel rejected. I need you to come over. Can you come now?" When this occurs I must decide where my own responsibility ends and where my friend's begins.

Individual Responsibility

The Bible is so encouraging as it helps us understand these principles of individual responsibility. In Romans 14:12 we are reminded that "each man shall give account of *himself* before God." You will be accountable for your *own* actions—not anyone else's reactions. And think for a moment about The Living Bible's translation of Ezekiel 18:20:

> The one who sins is the one who dies.
> The son shall not be punished for his
> father's sins, nor the father for his son's.
> The righteous person will be rewarded
> for his own goodness, and the wicked
> person for his own wickedness.

Each of us parents is responsible *to* "train up his child in the way he should go" (Proverbs 22:6). We are to teach the child the fear of the Lord, *to* love the child. *To* care for the child. But parents are *not* responsible *for* the actions of their grown children, nor for their choices and behavior! (Worried parents, heave a deep sigh of relief!)

My friend Margie's eyes began to fill with light. After we talked about these things she said, "You mean I am not responsible for the fact that my husband left me? I've always thought it was because I wasn't a good enough wife! Now you're saying that I'm not responsible for his choices? I see what you mean, Lee! I really was responsible *to* him, as best I could be. But I'm not held responsible *for* what he did. Thank God!"

Our neighbor Bill caught his son stealing again, back at some old tricks. Bill, Jr., whirled around and began to blast his father: "I wouldn't have these problems if you and Mom hadn't split up! We've never had any money to do anything. And you were never around when I needed you!"

After regaining his composure, Bill responded to his son, "Son, you're older now, and I can't take the responsibility for what you choose to do. I can't take the credit for your good, and I can't take the blame for your bad. I can't make your decisions for you or be responsible for their outcome. It's reached a point now where you'll have to make your choices and suffer your own consequences. I just hope you'll soon realize the importance of experiencing God's love and guidance for your life."

You said it, Dad! I wish every mom and dad who feels like a parental failure could learn they are responsible *to* and not *for* their children. The father of the prodigal son realized this. He didn't argue with his prodigal son when he wanted to leave home. He didn't put on sackcloth and ashes moaning, "Where did I go wrong?"

The dad rightly *let the son bear the burden of his own foolish choices.* And because he did, the prodigal returned home and was restored! The father followed God's own parenting example. For children who will not listen to His counsel He says: "I will let them eat of the fruit of their own ways and be filled with their own devices" (Proverbs 1:31).

So what is the solution to our present dissatisfaction?

"Stop and smell the roses" is just a cliche, but it is a powerful concept. Even happy but hectic schedules may contribute to a dull sense of discontent: "Once I get this book written, *then* I'll be able to relax a little!"

Like you, I have to remember that today is the day God has made for me. No "if onlys" can plague the mind of the woman who truly believes that God is in control of her life.

Second, we needn't allow other people to impose their moods and miseries upon us. No one can "make us" mad, sad, or bad. With God's help we choose our own emotions. And as we are filled with His Spirit, He will react through us. We'll see other people through *His* eyes.

And third, we are not responsible *for* other people. As Christians we are responsible only to allow God's blessings and gifts to flow *from* Him, *through* us, *to* our families, friends, and brothers and sisters in the body of Christ—His church. In this way we'll all grow together in His love.

To sum up the present, it's all we have! We needn't see ourselves as barefoot Cinderellas, always wondering where the glass slipper could be. "*This* is the day that the Lord has made . . . I will rejoice and be glad in it." Yesterday is a faded memory, worthy only of its lessons.

And tomorrow? I hope you're not living *there*! It's never-never land! "Tomorrow never comes," a song says; "there's just today." Yet unfortunately the future is one of the places where countless Cinderellas are waiting . . . forever waiting and watching. For the fairy godmother. For the prince. For the "happily-ever-after."

Chapter Seven

The Future—
When You Wish Upon A Star

"When you wish upon a star, your dreams come true."

Well, sorry, but it just isn't so—not for our past, not for our present, and definitely not for our future. We need something more solid than stargazing to get us through. Just ask Gina.

Our divorcee from Chapter 3, Gina, lived in constant fear of the future. Her past had been heartbreaking—her husband had left her for another woman. Her present was exhausting— trying to provide for her little brood of babies without time to really care for them. How could the future be anything but a disaster?

When I first met her, I was amazed by Gina's strength of character. She had incredible commitment to care for her children at all costs. And her battle was not only with fear for their future, but with guilt. She didn't feel like a good mother. Her little ones needed *her*, not just her paycheck.

We talked about the dilemma of the single parent. "Lee, it's a no-win situation. I'm damned if I do and damned if I don't. The family has to eat, and yet in the process of earning a living I'm neglecting the kids emotionally. What am I gonna do?"

"Gina, in your thinking does God fit into the picture anywhere?"

"Well, sure. I pray. But what's He gonna do about my problems? That's why He put me here—to take care of my kids. That's what mothers are for."

"But He wants to help you with the job."

"How can He help me? Send money in the mail?"

Gina and I talked for a long time. Although she had been brought up in a Catholic home, she had never understood that she could have a friendship with Jesus, that He cared about her personally.

"I thought He already lived in my heart!" She spoke with amazement when I asked her if she had ever actually invited Him into her life. "I thought He came inside when I was baptized."

"No, Gina, Christ wants you to ask Him into your life in an adult, choosing way. It's wonderful that your parents made the choice for you as a baby. But now it's up to you."

"What do I say?" A frown furrowed her forehead. But there was a glimmer of hope in her brown eyes.

"Just ask Him! Say, 'Jesus, please forgive my sins—please come and live in my heart. I want You to help me with my life, to take charge of my future and my kids' future too.' "

We prayed together. Happy tears bathed her face. By the time we parted she was radiant.

A few weeks later I called her to see how she was doing. "Well, I'm not rich yet!" she laughed. "No money in the mail!" But through some new friends, Gina found a Christian day-care center. Not only were her kids being cared for while she worked, but they were being taught about the Lord. And she was required to pay only as much as she could afford.

"What a load off my mind!" she sighed happily. "And we've all started praying every night together too. It's given me so much peace of mind. When I find myself worrying, I just ask Jesus to take over the problem. I can't believe the difference in the way I feel! I'm so much more motivated. I even cleaned my house Saturday!"

We Cinderella-hopefuls have no mice to help us sweep the floors clean; we have no birds to help us hang up the clothes on the line to dry. But when we discover a new inner motivation, it changes our outward attitude, and our actions soon follow suit.

The peace and joy which Gina experienced came from *faith*—a newfound faith in the God of the universe, in His deep and personal love. But what is faith?

Finding Faith

The Bible defines it for us: "Faith is the substance of things hoped for, the evidence of things not seen" (Hebrews 11:1 KJV). Faith involves both the future and the invisible—it is the guarantee and proof of both. In other words, faith is the *one* thing (tangible, solid, real) that we have to hold on to with regard to tomorrow.

Of course we may be "hopeful." And hope is a good thing. But hope is not faith. And it can get all tangled up with daydreaming.

Faith involves reality—the "now." And it's either going to have to be faith in ourselves or else a trusting faith in Jesus. Since we've pretty well concluded that we ourselves aren't a very good bet for winning the race alone, we had better put our faith in the One who has already beat the opposition! But how do we begin?

Faith is born when we accept the eloquent message of John 3:16: "For God so loved the world that He gave His only begotten Son, that whoever believes in Him should not perish but have everlasting life" (NKJV).

Simple? Childlike? Yes! And that's the beauty of it all. Jesus Christ *really did die for us*—for our past, our present, and our future. Have you asked Him to take control of the rest of your life?

"Trust in the Lord with all your heart, and lean not on your own understanding" (Proverbs 3:5 NKJV). All your tomorrows are secure in God. So dust off that old family Bible. It's got some good news inside!

Our faith in God should become an hour-by-hour happening. Hebrews 11:6 tells us that "without faith it is impossible to please God." Like Gina, let's develop a practical reliance on Christ. Jesus said in Mark 9:23, "All things are possible to him who believes" (NKJV). Faith is an active thing—a trusting, a knowing, a growing inside us—even if, to begin with, our faith is as small as a grain of mustard seed.

Faith is especially important to Cinderella thinkers because it has the power to "cast down imaginations" and to "bring into captivity every thought to the obedience of Christ" (2 Corinthians 10:5 KJV). What kind of "imaginations" do we cling to? Are we . . .

Imagining that we'll enjoy a more prosperous life someday?

Imagining that eventually the people close to us will change?

Imagining that Mr. Right will come along soon?

Faith is the "substance" that helps us discover God's plan when our own dreams don't come true. Faith is the promise that He will take care of us no matter what the circumstances. Faith *is* the future, unseen and yet more real than reality itself!

But what does faith actually change? How is our future affected when we surrender to Christ? No more problems? Not necessarily. Not always. Not likely. Upon stepping into a life of faith, our everyday world won't be transformed by some unseen magic.

But we will begin to realize that our capacity to make right choices has been altered. And we will discover that the love and grace of God are greater than any need or problem we could possibly fear.

There's an old adage: "Prayer changes things." This seems to vaguely suggest that everything will be rosy in the future if we simply pray. I have seen many situations revolutionized through prayer—no question about it. But there is something deeper to be understood here.

It is far more accurate to say, "Prayer changes *people*." How wonderful! *Even without altering our outward environment, prayer can renew us on the inside.* It can give us a totally new perspective of everything.

No Goals?

But what does this mean? If we realize contentment and satisfaction in our present situation, do we resign ourselves to mediocrity or passivity? Not at all! In the midst of peace and satisfaction we can be sure that God has even better things in store for tomorrow. And we are certainly free to have plans of our own, as long as we submit them to God's scrutiny and possible veto.

First of all, there are two kinds of ideas—good and bad, realistic and impractical. Let's spend a few moments with some women who are about to take a close look at their hearts' desires. Maybe they can show us how to find our own way from the shadows of daydreaming into the full light of reality.

Joan's deepest longing is to travel to Europe. There she sits in the cozy corner of her favorite cafe, sipping hot coffee, absorbed in a stack of travel guides, brochures, and maps. A faraway look is in her eyes. A smile flickers around the corners of her mouth. Excitement surges inside her.

Karen really wants to lose 50 pounds. (And she really needs to!) Bravely standing in front of her full-length mirror, she's garbed in nothing but panties and a bra. Unmercifully she confronts her lumps, bumps, and ripples. She's on the verge of tears.

Linda feels she would like to write her own book. After skimming several personal testimony titles in the Christian bookstore, she senses that a story like hers has yet to be told. A strange, inner drive begins to stir up her thoughts.

At this point in our projects, along with our heroines, each of us needs to ask herself the same three questions:

- Do I have the control or responsibility necessary to make this scheme come to pass?

- Do I have the required skill and energy to complete this endeavor?
- With God's help, can I prepare myself adequately for the task?

"Delight yourself in the Lord," promises the psalmist, "and He will give you the desires of your heart" (Psalm 37:4). Ever think about that?

Maybe He's the one who put the idea in your head in the first place. If that's the case, the answer to all three questions will be *yes*. And once we've all sorted out the fake fantasies and hung on to some genuine goals, we have work to do. We begin carving out contentment before we realize our goals.

Joan begins calling travel agents. She lists the actual costs of a European adventure. After talking to friends who have made the journey themselves, she tentatively plots her itinerary, opens a savings account, and applies for a passport.

Karen investigates Weight Watchers, calorie-counting, and the reducing plan offered by a local health club. She buys a bathroom scale, gives away her bag of sugar, stops hoarding snack food, and seeks to develop better eating habits.

Linda writes several inquiry letters to publishers. She begins to jot down ideas. Her reading time increases as she attempts to learn how others have told their tales. She outlines her chapters, sketches out a synopsis, and locates a typist.

How about us? How can we "make it happen"? By listing our options, assessing our agendas, and staking out our strategies. But let's remember, "The mind of man plans his way, but the Lord directs his steps" (Proverbs 16:9 NASB).

As our efforts increase, each of us makes conscious choices about attitude. It's uplifting to accentuate the positive aspects along the way. "Whistle while you work," chanted the seven dwarves, and for once a fairy tale makes a good suggestion.

By now Joan is fighting dissatisfaction with "everyday" life. Anticipating her exciting trip, she is struggling with impatience and boredom. "Sometimes the hands of the clock never seem to move!" she sighs. "But at least I've got time to get things in order. And people say that half the fun is making plans!"

Meanwhile Karen is frustrated—her bathroom scale has been stuck on the same weight for a week. It's a daily struggle to stick to her new regimen, with discouragement nagging at her constantly. "Well, thank God I'm not *gaining weight*," Karen smiles a little sadly. "And I sure am learning a thing or two about patience!"

> Whatever is true, honorable, or just;
> Whatever is pure, lovely, or gracious;
> If there is any excellence,
> Or anything worthy of praise,
> *Think about these things!* (Philippians 4:8).

Soon-to-be-author Linda feels almost helpless as she tries to record her unique history. The story is actually falling into place very nicely. It's just that there aren't enough hours in the day. After working all day and confronting her household duties at night, she's almost too weary to face the typewriter. "And yet I have this weird feeling that I've *got to write this book*! It's like a sense of mission or something. . .I don't know what it is, but it keeps me going!"

By concentrating on our present blessings even as we work toward something better, we can't help but be contented. But if we're contented, isn't it inconsistent to have high hopes for tomorrow? Contentment doesn't mean overjoyed. Neither does it mean resigned. We are free to hope and trust and believe. And it can be done without our falling back into the Cinderella Syndrome.

Different Reactions

This is a good opportunity for us to take a close look at our temperaments in relation to our view of the future.

The strong-leader-type, the *Choleric* temperament, tends to dream and to disguise those fantasy-longings as "goals." All too often she will be setting these goals much too high for herself as well as for others. Her wishes stretch well beyond the reach of reality.

The *Phlegmatic* temperament has a more laid-back personality. She is not a superachiever, and tends to dream rather than act. She feels she's a victim of circumstances. There's nothing she can do to change things, so she winds up being an observer of life rather than a participant.

The temperament that gets most excited about her dreams is the *Sanguine*. Because she naturally believes that "tomorrow will be a better day," she may even lie to herself, as well as to others, that her dreams are about to come true!

The personalities most prone to fantasy-thinking are those with a touch of *Melancholy* in their temperament blend. These introspective souls tend to fantasize rather than make progress. She believes it is her "cross" to learn to "cope," so she resigns herself to a miserable life. She may even develop a slight martyr complex in the process.

No matter what temperament we claim, our dreams must be firmly founded on something stronger than wishful thinking. If our lives are truly centered on Christ and His desire for our well-being, then hope can keep us growing. The ultimate example of this is the "blessed hope of the church"—the return of Jesus. It is based on God's own promise. It's a sure bet. Yet, in the meantime, we are instructed to faithfully "occupy until He comes" (Luke 19:13).

Breaking the Cycle

So let's break the vicious cycle put in motion by Cinderella thinking:

ANTICIPATION → FRUSTRATION → DEPRESSION →

The more we anticipate a happening, the more frustration we will feel in our lives. Instead, let's *test our dreams,* plan a strategy, rejoice as we make our best efforts, and nurture the faith that God has planted in our hearts.

"Just who is it that we're putting all this faith in?" you're probably wondering by now. "What kind of a God have I entrusted with my precious tomorrows? Does He really care about ordinary people like me?"

One sunny afternoon the King of Kings and Lord of Lords sat on a Galilean hillside with His disciples. They were surrounded by pleasant country landscapes—wildflowers, happily chirping sparrows, and the colorful crowds that clung to the Master's every word.

> Look at the birds of the air . . . . They do not sow, neither do they reap, nor gather into barns, and yet your heavenly Father feeds them. Are you not worth much more than they? . . .
>
> And why are you anxious about clothing? Observe how the lilies of the field grow; they do not toil nor do they spin, yet I say to you that even Solomon in all his glory did not clothe himself like one of these. But if God so arrays the grass of the field, which is alive today and tomorrow is thrown into the furnace, will He not much more do so for you, O men of little faith?
>
> Do not be anxious then, saying,

"What shall we eat?" or "What shall we drink?" or "With what shall we clothe ourselves?" . . . for your heavenly Father knows that you need all these things. But seek first His kingdom and His righteousness, and all these things shall be added to you.

Therefore do not be anxious for tomorrow; for tomorrow will care for itself. Each day has enough trouble of its own (Matthew 6:26, 28-34 NASB).

What is it that we're so worried about? Money? Success? Old age? Status? Ill-health? Catastrophe? Heartbreak? Disappointment? Death?

"For I know the plans I have for you," declares our wonderful, caring Lord, "plans for good and not for evil to give you a future, and a hope" (Jeremiah 29:11 TLB). For some of us who have been Christians for a while, it takes only a backward glance now and then to see how very true these beautiful promises really are.

Sylvia, a lovely woman I first met at a seminar, revealed to me her own view of the future. "I sure don't believe in living in the past," she smiled. "But I never want to lose sight of what God has done in my life, either."

Sylvia was a petite, silver-haired woman who at first gave the impression that she had never had a moment of difficulty. But as we stood talking beside a sunlit window, I learned that she and her husband had traveled many a rocky road together.

"I have a list in my desk," Sylvia explained, "on which I've recorded every miracle, every answered prayer, and every victory that God has ever accomplished in our lives. I keep it up-to-date. And when I remember something else I add it immediately."

"What's it for?" I asked her, fairly sure I knew what she was about to tell me.

"When things get tough I get out the list. And I go over it point-by-point. 'Thank You, Jesus, for this,' I pray. 'Thank You, Jesus, for that.' By the time I'm through, I *know* He's got the future well in hand—He's never failed me yet!"

In Joshua chapter 4 the wise leader of the Israelites instructed his people to take 12 stones from the middle of the Jordan River, which God had miraculously parted. "Make a memorial," said Joshua, "so that when your children ask later, 'What do these stones mean to you?' you shall say to them, 'The waters of the Jordan were cut off before the ark of the covenant of the Lord . . . these stones are a memorial to the sons of Israel forever.' "

We have a responsibility before God to never forget the glorious things He has done for us in the past. It is often His past provision that gives us the greatest hope for the future!

Future Parenting

And we have the pleasant responsibility of sharing those "memorials" with our children, just as Joshua admonished the people to do long ago.

Bible stories are important. But *personal* accounts of God's present love are also vital to our children's spiritual understanding.

As a new Christian, Gina learned that she had a spiritual duty to her children. This same joy involves all us mothers. And it includes protecting our kids from the Cinderella Syndrome! Perhaps in the future they won't have to struggle (as some of us have) with unrealistic thinking. We can begin by immunizing them with "personal responsibility" vaccine.

By teaching kids to be accountable for themselves, to deal with their own consequences, we prepare them for a less-than-fairytale-perfect life. If we want our children to keep their feet on the ground, we must put some responsibility on their shoulders!

Furthermore, we should spiritually educate them about life. Let's slowly phase ourselves out of the position of "savior" for them. The sooner kids learn they can trust in the Lord themselves, the sooner they cultivate a strong faith of their own.

After all, the goal of every person alive should be inner strength and freedom in Christ. God has provided a way for each of us to emancipate ourselves from within, without the intervention of some external magic. As mothers, let's ask ourselves, "Does my child feel like he or she can make it without me? Have I taught him or her to depend on God for the future?"

As the saying goes, there are two lasting things we must give our children—one is roots, the other is wings. At my house, we raise small birds in an aviary off our bedroom window. These cheerful, feathered friends have taught me many lessons about raising my own children.

Occasionally I see a mother bird launch her children into flight by simply pushing them out of the nest! *Surely,* I say to myself, *she would prefer snuggling with them in the safe, comfortable home rather than watching them dash themselves into the walls!* Nevertheless, push she does! And they do learn!

Mothers sigh, "Sure they can fly! But always in the wrong direction!" Our children *may* choose the last course we would like them to follow. Yet it is our duty to equip them with strong wings. They must find their way alone, secure with God, without a crippling dependency upon Mom or Dad. We all must face up to our responsibilities, which brings a story to mind.

> The dutiful mother ripped off the covers for the third time.
>
> "You *have* to go to church," she insisted.
>
> "But I don't want to go to church," the sleeper replied.
>
> "You have no choice; you *must* go to church," she answered.
>
> "But *why*?"
>
> "Because you are 38 years old, and you are the pastor!"

Future Worries?

In her book *The Hiding Place* Corrie ten Boom found herself worried about her future. How could she be true to Christ if she were dragged away to a concentration camp? Her wise old father smiled at her, his eyes twinkling.

"Corrie, when Papa takes you to the train station, when does he give you your ticket?"

Corrie responded, "Just before I have to board the train, Papa."

He nodded, "And so will God the Father!"

Is there a coming "train" you've been trying to board without having yet received your ticket? We've been assured (1 Corinthians 10:13) that we will not be tempted beyond what we can stand. God will graciously give us the very ticket we need—His grace—for any future train that may pull into our station.

One of my goals in life is to be a sweet old lady. That may sound a little strange, but I've met some rocking-chair occupants who are definitely not of the cheerful, friendly variety. Colette Dowling says in *The Cinderella Complex:*

> The devastation of old age is the most poignant outcome of the Cinderella Complex, if not the most destructive. . . . We want so desperately to believe that someone else will take care of us. We want so desperately to believe that we do not have to be responsible for our own welfare (p. 49).

What *do* we have to look forward to? The Bible says, "A gray head is a crown of glory; it is found in *the way of righteousness*" (Proverbs 16:31 NASB). I believe anyone can be serene and beloved in those declining years by developing good habits *now*.

In choosing *forgiveness*, we can avoid the resentful, angry, and bitter emotions that sometimes poison the elderly. In choosing freedom from depending on other people today, we can find satisfaction and contentment in our old age. In choosing to develop our *faith* in Christ we are assured of peace as we confront the very special difficulties that only the aging can fully understand.

And without believing a "fairy tale," by faith we can know that *God* will take care of us then. We can rest peacefully with the confidence that *He* will be responsible for our welfare. Tomorrow belongs only to *Him*.

Meanwhile, consider the words of C. S. Lewis:

> Never commit your happiness to the future. Happy work is best done by the man who takes his longterm plans somewhat lightly and works from moment to moment as to the Lord. The present is the only item in which any duty can be done, or any grace received.

Forgiveness is the golden key to the past. Freedom from the tyranny of other people is the silver key to the present. Faith is the bejeweled key to a hopeful, glorious future.

But there is one more dreary prison to be unlocked—one more sturdy steel key to be turned. And it may be the most important of them all. Without it you'll never depart the Cinderella Syndrome's fairytale tower. I know—I myself almost stayed there forever-after.

Chapter Eight

The Key To Escape

A fly buzzed against the window as I tried to redirect my attention toward Shirley's Bible class. My mind had been drowsily wandering in the lazy summer heat to thoughts of Hal and his two complex daughters. Suddenly Shirley's words startled me like ice water splashed against my warm face.

"You hold the key to your own happiness," she was saying somewhat matter-of-factly.

It's unfair, I fumed silently. *I'm tired of being responsible for everything—the kids, the house, the dog, remembering birthdays. Now you expect me to be the key to my own happiness, too?*

Shirley had certainly touched a sensitive spot in *my* world. By the time I had stopped waiting for my happiness to arrive with marriage and a lovely home, I had begun looking to Hal to make me content. I was waiting for his daughters to accept me as yet another mom, waiting for all our differences to resolve themselves. Clearly these methods weren't working too well. I assumed that God was withholding my happiness like the Internal Revenue Service withholds our taxes. Was He keeping it from me until I could prove to Him I deserved it?

"Jesus is the key to *my* happiness," I informed the teacher piously that day in class.

"No, He is not." She smiled knowingly.

Heresy! Blasphemy! "Are you trying to tell me that God cannot make me happy?" I spluttered indignantly.

"Of course God *can* make you happy! But since He has already given you everything you could possibly need, whose fault is it if you aren't enjoying life?"

For the first time in my memory, I realized that I had no one to blame for my problems but *me*!

Turning The Key

Let's pretend for a moment that God came to your house and gave you a brand-new, late-model car. "This is a gift for you," He announces, "and here are the keys."

"Thanks a million, Lord! What a dynamite gift!"

The second He's out of sight, you rush outside and fully check this baby out. "Wow!" you say. "This is a terrific car! I'm gonna take it for a spin!"

You hop in the driver's seat, and then what do you do? You don't pray for God to perform yet another miracle and turn over the engine. You don't wait for someone else to come and hot-wire it. You don't get irritated at the dumb car because it won't start on its own. You don't hope God will send you a smarter car. *You just turn the key and the car starts.*

If you can't get the car started, whose fault is it? It's not someone else's fault—why would God give him or her the key to *your* car? And it's not God's fault—He already gave you the key. Here's the point: *That car is your own happiness, and the key is pocketed inside your own will.*

There's a saying that states, "Happiness is not a *destination,* but a *journey.*" It is a process, a path, a road we travel. This too fits in with the car analogy. When we plan an excursion and a friend asks, "Where are you going?" we don't say, "We're just going to the car for a few days."

The car is not the destination but *the means* we employ to get where we want to go. Being in the car—being happy—is part of the journey, part of the process of living. I will never get out of my car, take a look around, and say, "Well, here we are, folks, Happyland!" Happyland is like the pot at the end of the rainbow, or the cloud with the silver lining. These are *concepts,* not *locations.*

What is happiness, anyway? Is it a sense of girlish glee? A giggling emotional high? A constant emotional fireworks show?

Adult happiness, in a Christian context, is peace of mind, contentment, a quiet inner spirit that is blessed with the joyful awareness of God's constant love and blessing.

> Praise the Lord! For all who fear God and trust in Him are blessed beyond expression. Yes, happy is the man who delights in doing his commands (Psalm 112:1 TLB).

> You will show me the path that leads to life; your presence fills me with joy and brings me pleasure forever (Psalm 16:11 TEV).

> We are able to hold our heads high no matter what happens and know that all is well, for we know how dearly God loves us, and we feel this warm love everywhere within us because God has given us the Holy Spirit to fill our hearts with his love (Romans 5:5 TLB).

With promises such as these made especially to us, it's obviously incumbent upon each of us to take one healthy dose of personal responsibility every morning. As speaker Patsy Clairmont says, we need to make a decision to wake up and say, "Good morning, Lord!" rather than "Good Lord, it's morning!"

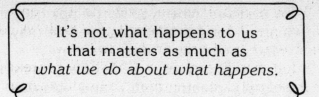

It's not what happens to us
that matters as much as
what we do about what happens.

We needn't depend on our circumstances to make us happy. We can elect to be happy no matter what's going on. We *choose* our emotions— they are not thrust upon us by some unseen force.

We must develop new patterns of thinking and new habits of behavior. It's a little like passing a driving test before receiving a license: There are some rules we must follow before we can be legally permitted to drive our "happiness vehicles" along life's bumpy, rocky highway.

Rules of the Road

1. *Pray for God's assistance!* He realizes that you're attempting to change, and He will navigate you through the detours, obstacles, and potholes ahead. Proverbs 3:6 reminds us, "In all your ways acknowledge Him, and He will direct your paths."
2. *Single out the one or two persons* on whom you most depend for your happiness. Announce to them that they are not responsible for you anymore—that you're not a backseat driver anymore but have discovered that you own a car of your own! (Often just saying this out loud will help you abide

by the rules. When you start slipping up and leaning too heavily, these people may remind you of your new "freedom".)

3. *Get a key*, any key, made of any material (metal, plastic, etc.) and display it somewhere in your home or office. If you can find a little "charm" key, wear it. Let it remind you, "I hold the key to my own happiness."

4. *Speak and act cheerfully.* "A merry heart does good like a medicine" (Proverbs 17:22). Give of yourself; give cheer, not sarcasm. Be positive, not negative. "Be thankful in all things" (1 Thessalonians 5:18) is more than a cliche; it is a perspective of faith—of believing that God is in charge and that He has our best interest at heart.

Growing Up with the Syndrome

One reason so many of us have had problems taking the responsibility for our own emotional well-being may lie in childhood. Dependency is a natural part of the early years. As small children we are trained to depend on Mommy for our happiness. Mommy cheers us up when we are sad. Mommy holds us when we are scared of the dark. Mommy has the answers to all our questions and beams with approval when we do well. Before we even get to kindergarten, we may have concluded that someone else brings us happiness!

In grammar school we are sometimes bored or listless. School is a drag; no one treats us as well as Mommy does. Meanwhile, Mommy always makes the extra effort to cheer us up by fixing us special lunches or by helping us with our toughest homework.

In junior high we aren't so dependent on Mommy for advice. Now we're old enough to figure things out for ourselves. With great worldly wisdom we say, "I *hate* being 12. I can't wait till I'm a teenager." Or we say, "Being 14 is the pits! When I can drive, everything will be better." But once we get the driver's license we say, "When I'm 18, and in college, I'll have it made."

Occasionally we read in magazines and newspapers about men and women who pursued happiness full-speed. Whether they wanted fame, fortune, love, or status, they worked and fought until that dream came true. But when they finally got "it," they still weren't happy and drowned their despair in alcohol or drugs.

Where does it all end? Have we ever *really* grown up? Do we still find ourselves counting on some outside person or external force to trigger our happiness? Have we learned that peace and contentment spring from an internal well? And do we know what that artesian fountain really is?

After all is said and done, relationships are truly the only things that really matter. Almost everything else in our lives is done to be undone. We prepare a meal and watch the family instantly devour it. We wash the dog just in time for her to run out and roll in the mud. We make the bed and in a few hours we're only too glad to crawl back into it again. Only relationships are meant to last.

I made this statement at a seminar once and a young lady immediately scowled and thrust her hand into the air. "But, *Lee*! I thought you just said we're not supposed to look for happiness in other people. I don't get it! What are you trying to say?"

The woman heard me right—both times. We *can't* expect others to make us happy. But we are called to be servants to them, to pray for them. None of this is intended to please them, to "buy" their affection so they'll make us happy. No, it's a matter of obedience. And obedience makes *God* happy.

Let's not wait to be "loved" anymore; let's begin loving! Let's not long to be "cared for"; let's begin caring. Let's not wish somebody would fall down and die for us; let's lay down our lives for our friends and families, our neighbors and co-workers.

Take the risk! By now you've cleared the effects of your past through forgiveness. You know you can enjoy freedom from manipulation in the present. You're looking toward your future with faith and trust in God. So begin to "lose" your life. You'll surely find it. And you won't need a course in the power of positive thinking to appreciate what you have, either.

Just Think Positive?

"Positive Mental Attitude" is big business

today. Seminars abound. Books line the library shelves. Tapes talk to us whether we're awake or asleep. "Love yourself!" we're commanded. "Keep your sunny side up! Don't utter a negative word! Rah! Rah!"

Unfortunately, the usual source of self-esteem is a sort of deified "Self" with unlimited human potential. If God is included in any of this, it's usually as a benevolent old celestial wonder-worker who rewards the positive-minded and withholds anything good from those who possess the dreaded, forbidden "negative outlook."

No positive-thinking doctrine alone is enough to change our lives. Such answers are equivalent to trying to pull yourself up by your own boot-straps. It doesn't work—gravity gets in the way!

In order to raise ourselves up, we must have at least one hand firmly fixed on a solid object higher than ourselves. We need to ask ourselves, "Do I have a firm grip on God? Am I leaning on His power to help pull me out of my muddy, miry existence?"

The Bible has its own positive perspective, always based on praise and thanksgiving to a generous heavenly Father. The Bible says that all our valuable potential is in Him, by the power of His Son.

As for techniques? They couldn't be more simple:

> Rejoice in the Lord always; again I will say, rejoice! Let your forbearing spirit be known to all men. The Lord is near. Be

anxious for nothing, but in everything by prayer and supplication with thanksgiving let your requests be made known to God. And the peace of God, which surpasses all comprehension, shall guard your hearts and your minds in Christ Jesus.

Finally, brethren, whatever is true, whatever is honorable, whatever is right, whatever is pure, whatever is lovely, whatever is of good report, if there is any excellence and if anything worthy of praise, *let your mind dwell on these things* (Philippians 4:4-8 NASB).

Kathy arrived at our Bible study a little late. She quickly sat down in the back row and focused her attention on what was being said. I couldn't help but notice the sweet expressions that fleeted across her young face from time to time.

A few months before, she had started coming to our women's group. And she was a far different woman today from the one she had been when we first got to know her. At that time anger had often flashed in her clear blue eyes, and beneath them dark circles spoke of her deep inner exhaustion.

After several brief conversations, I had learned that Kathy was the weary mother of two children with special challenges: one severely retarded and one with a puzzling, chronic reading disability. She was a Christian, yes. Some longing for help had kept her coming to these strengthening times of fellowship. But she was seething in her spirit. As far as she was concerned, God had given her more than her portion of pain.

Not one of us could disagree. "*Why?*" Kathy asked me one day, fighting back tears. "I *asked* Him to let my second baby be okay. I *begged* Him. And I believed. I really did. So *why?*"

What could I say to her? Any problems I had ever faced vanished when contrasted with the ceaseless struggle Kathy lived with.

"I don't have an answer to that question, Kathy. Nobody on this earth does. All I can tell you is that, barring a miracle, your circumstances aren't going to change. Somehow, someway, you've got to find a means of being peaceful *within* those terrible circumstances."

"Oh, really? Well, *you* try it!" she had snapped at me and turned away. Over the course of some weeks our group had been searching out the problems of the past, the present, and the future which might be crippling us. And eventually we tackled the matter of "The Key."

"You are responsible for your own happiness!" My own words echoed in my memory, and I cringed a little recalling how that statement had infuriated *me!*

Kathy had said nothing to me after class. But in the weeks to come we all began to notice subtle changes in her demeanor. She smiled more frequently. She even laughed now and then.

"What's happened to you, Kathy?" I bravely questioned her at last, no longer able to contain my curiosity.

"I guess I've just learned how to be thankful, Lee. The idea that I was responsible for my own happiness really made me stop and count my blessings. And now, every time I get on the emotional skids, I try to remember to thank God *out loud* for every single good thing that I can possibly think of!

"That verse from Philippians 4 really set me on the right track. In fact I've memorized it now: 'Finally, brethren, whatever things are true, honest, just, pure, lovely, of good report, if there is any virtue, any praise, *think on these things!*"

Kathy paused, and I stared at her, marveling at her simple faith.

"And you know what?" she went on, with a beautiful smile on her face. "In spite of everything—and I mean *everything*—there's a whole lot more good in my life than there is bad!"

The kids sing it in Sunday school. Remember? "I've got the peace that passes understanding down in my heart...down in my heart to stay." At last Kathy's got it. Lee's got it too.

How about you?

If life is a journey,
then life's greatest tragedy
is not having enjoyed the trip.

Chapter Nine

A Delicate Balance

The dazzling spotlight set her sequined costume aflame like a shaft of shimmering diamonds. I watched her breathlessly as she carefully, skillfully made her way across the tightrope. The drum roll crescendoed.

No net assured her of a safe landing. Only her own expertise guaranteed that she would reach the other platform safely. High, high above the arena floor she performed her amazing feats—handstands, pirouettes, backward flips.

Like a beautiful lightning bug she danced and dipped to the delight of us all. And she never so much as wavered. Her sense of balance was as spectacular as her glittering, gleaming form. When her act was completed the rapt audience exploded into cascades of applause.

Our search for happiness in our present circumstance will fail without a solid relationship with God through Jesus Christ. The Cinderella Syndrome won't be cured without Him. But attaining a proper balance of responsibility between ourselves and God is also crucial. And like a well-rehearsed circus performer, at times we must tiptoe across a narrow and tricky course.

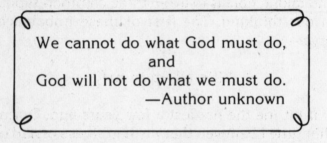

> We cannot do what God must do,
> and
> God will not do what we must do.
> —Author unknown

Don't be misled. The little poem doesn't say, "God *cannot* do what we must do." Certainly, God *can* do anything. If He wanted to He could wipe away all our present problems and turn earth into heaven for all of us.

Have you ever toiled in prayer half the night only to wake up to the same unrelenting heartache? When that happens, we are left with two alternatives. Since we can't conclude that God is impotent—simply unable to do what we've asked—we must resign ourselves to the fact that He has a reason for letting things stay as they are. Or we can deduce that He is leaving part of the job up to us!

No doubt you've heard the often-quoted prayer:

> God grant me the serenity
> To accept the things I cannot change,
> The courage to change the things I can,
> And the wisdom to know the difference.

In this simple request lies the delicate balance that we're talking about. Herein is true freedom from the Cinderella Syndrome. To begin to understand the relationship between letting go and taking hold is to avoid three common slipups in our thinking. The first of these imbalances says—

"It's all up to me"

It hit me the hardest a few years ago. During that time I believed that my happiness rested on the strength of my own faith. When I was "up" and inspired, I credited my faith. When I was down and blue, I blamed by lack of faith. I didn't see it as such, but I was trusting in "works" alone. When I couldn't see "fruit" I figured I was at fault for some mysterious lack of spirituality.

If I found myself unhappy or discontented (as I often did) I scolded myself for not "claiming the victory," for not "believing" strongly enough in God. I kept "confessing" what I wanted God to do for me.

I was overly reliant on my "quiet time." If I missed "morning devotion," I assumed I had blown another day. "If only I read the Bible more," I said to myself. "If only I spent more time in prayer, *then* my life would fall into place." When this "cramming for exams" period ended, I emerged full of biblical knowledge, having logged more prayer hours than ever before. Yet I still wasn't content with my life.

Of course, reading our Bibles and talking with God are important activities. And they *will* strengthen our faith in Him. But we simply *cannot rely on our spirituality* alone to make us happy.

Along the same lines, "It's all up to me" can fall into the "God helps him who helps himself" cliche. There *are* many things we can do. But there are times when God clearly says, "Leave it alone." "Wait." "Cease striving."

Are you a good spiritual listener? Am I? If you are a "doer," He may be teaching you to let Him handle the job in spite of your willingness to be His able-bodied assistant. Ruth 3:18 is good advice for some of us activists.

Wait, my daughter, until you know how
the matter turns out (NASB).

In Ruth's case it was up to Boaz, her eventual husband, to make the next move. And at times we need to let others do their part without manipulating them, without nagging them. We need to wait patiently and contentedly, for them to act.

But here the balancing act grows extremely delicate again. For imbalance number two almost topples us over by saying—

"It's all up to you"

When you hold someone else accountable for your happiness, and you wait for that person to perform, you may be setting yourself up for inevitable disappointment and disillusionment. Even the most wonderful, near-perfect person in the world will eventually let you down.

My two daughters, like many teenagers, misbehaved, disobeyed, and rebelled against their parents during high school. To our dismay, they weren't turning out as we had planned! And today they won't deny that they were neither pleasant to spend time with nor the least bit lovable during those difficult years.

Part of my personal image seemed to rest on their angry young shoulders. It was hard enough trying to be a model stepmother when they were little kids. Now my entire reputation as a Christian leader was sliding down the tubes!

As I felt myself judged unfairly by our friends and fellow church members, a root of bitterness began to take root. I had trusted and relied on my daughters to perform in a manner that would make me proud and well-thought about. (Wasn't I supposed to be Supermom?) Instead, they were letting me down.

The problem was that my trust and reliance had been misplaced. Keeping my reputation spotless was far too big an order for my children to fill. Why is it that we parents expect our children to build parental self-esteem? I don't know, but I see it happening all the time, and I have been guilty of it myself.

I shudder when I hear a parent remark, "My children are my pride and joy." It simply is not our child's responsibility to make us happy or cause us to think better of ourselves. Certainly our offspring must carry the weight of *their own* happiness, but they are not built to carry their parents' as well.

This same myth sometimes affects our relationship with friends. Do we require our friends to keep close contact with us? Are we hurt when we see cliques forming without us? Do we feel let down when Gloria hasn't telephoned for five days in a row? Guess what? The telephone has two ends! *You* can reach out and touch someone too.

At work, do you let your moods swing right along with your bosses? Can you diligently and joyfully work even though your coworkers complain? Do I feel I must adopt my husband's miserable mood when he brings it home uninvited from the office?

The same problems occur when we expect others to accomplish things for us. A salty old man I know sometimes says, "If you want nothing done, let someone else do it!" How true!

Passing the proverbial buck of responsibility is a habit common to most of us. And the subsequent griping over a job half done or not done at all is just as familiar a turf.

Where does "delegation" stop and personal

responsibility start? Back we go listening to God again. Are you a pushy type taking on more than you can handle? Or are you a watcher, waiting for the "happening" to happen? As far as your own specific circumstances are concerned, what has God told you through His Word? His still, small voice?

My friend Carol once found herself living in a not-so-clean house. "When I get a little money together," she promised me, "I'm having this placed cleaned, and cleaned right!"

For several weeks a mythical cleaning lady lurked in the shadows, her mops and brooms poised for future activity.

Finally the cruel light of reality dawned when, after eyeing the dust curled in the corners, Carol's patient husband, Jim, inquired, "Aren't you *ever* going to clean this place again?"

"When I get a little money together," she informed him, "I'm hiring a cleaning woman."

Jim quietly reminded Carol of the family's less-than-plush financial situation.

Next time I talked to her she was frantically cleaning her house. "I guess it's up to me," she sheepishly informed me. "I'll have to clean the house myself this time. But *next* time I'm hiring a cleaning lady. Then the job will be done right!"

Sometimes we have the same problem with God. We expect Him to clean up our dirty little habit, to scrub up our ugly little sins. And we find ourselves teetering on the edge of imbalance number three—

"It's all up to God"

When I came to this slippery spot on the tightrope, I convinced myself that God would have to do *everything* that needed to be done. This vein of thinking paralyzed me and transformed me from an active participant to a passive observer in life. "Waiting on the Lord" became my life's work. Resentment against God began to well up inside. Why wasn't He making me more satisfied? He didn't seem to be holding up His end of the deal!

Discovering that "faith without works is dead" (according to James 2:17) destroyed this particular myth for me. It is not up to God to do all the work! We must establish the balance of responsibility with God. The two of us working together can move mountains. He will always hold up His end. But how about you? How about me?

In great measure God has already done His part by allowing His Son to live within the heart of everyone who asks and believes.

This balance of responsibility is not an "either/or" situation. We say, "Jesus is the Light of the world." Yet Jesus said, "*You* are the light of the world" (Matthew 5:14). He is sharing His responsibility with us. It's easy to believe that "Jesus has all power," but Jesus said, "Behold, I give *you* power" (Luke 10:19). He wants to distribute His kingdom authority through all who believe in Him.

Many people have developed an erroneous

concept of God as a sort of "divine Butler" whose job it is to serve us and bring us everything we want on a silver platter. Could it be that we are waiting for God to do something He is waiting for us to do?

A farmer who grew the most beautiful produce in the area took a visitor to see his fields. "My," exclaimed the man, "what beautiful produce God has made!"

"Yeah," drawled the farmer, "but you should have seen this field when God had it all by Himself!"

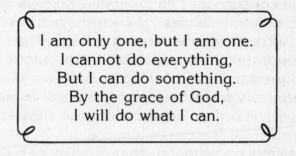

I am only one, but I am one.
I cannot do everything,
But I can do something.
By the grace of God,
I will do what I can.

Nancy didn't like carpooling, living in Maple Grove, California, feeding the dog, or cleaning her house. Sure, she liked being a mom. But she felt she wasn't really a very good one because she sometimes had to work on the weekends. "I just don't spend enough time with the children," she sighed.

What was poor Nancy to do? Pray? Wait on the Lord? Move? Divorce her family and become a feminist?

To begin with, Nancy had to establish a balance of responsibility; then she could start working on *her* share of the assignment.

Her first task was to *change her attitude* about the things that bothered her. Nancy prayed about her feelings. She consciously applied the Scripture found in Colossians 3:23: "Whatever you do, do it heartily, as to the Lord" (NKJV).

If Jesus were a member of the car pool, wouldn't Nancy enthusiastically volunteer to pick up the kids every day? If Christ lived in her neighborhood, would she be homesick for Iowa? If she considered her son's collie to be a gift from God, wouldn't Nancy more diligently care for it? If the Lord dropped by for coffee, (excuse me— herb tea) wouldn't Nancy want the beds made? And if Nancy truly believed that Jesus guided her as she parented her two children, wouldn't she find greater peace of mind?

After she prayerfully got her attitude in better shape, she began to realistically evaluate her circumstances. The carpooling couldn't be helped. And until her school district discovered money for increased bus routes, Nancy would have to joyfully cart kids to and from school three times a week. "But thank God I don't have to do it every day!" she chuckled.

Living in Maple Grove, away from her family and friends in Iowa, was a necessary part of her husband's job. Nancy began to consciously work at appreciating her new home, the mild climate, and the small-town atmosphere. And recently Nancy confessed to me that she wasn't really all that homesick anymore. "When God decides to move me, He will; until then, I'm going to be happy right where I live today!"

The housecleaning and pet care dilemmas were improved when Nancy began assigning more chores to her children. And by working a few extra hours a week herself she was able to hire a neighborhood teenager to help her around the house on Saturdays. "There are some jobs I really like," says Nancy, "but the ones I can't *tolerate* I *delegate*!"

Her doubts about being a good mom probably won't be resolved completely until her children are grown. But while she's waiting for a work schedule that will insure her weekends off, Nancy spends more time with each child individually. "Quality time" it's called in parenting literature. And quality time is far more important than a *quantity* of hours.

Getting her actions balanced with her attitude was Nancy's number one need. She handled it very well! And that same delicate balance is forever necessary to the "act" of living— for all of us. The spotlight is in place. The drums are rolling. The world is watching. Are we ready?

I cherish a little brass plaque I bought at a marine supply store several years ago. I think it sums up the "balance" in a superb way:

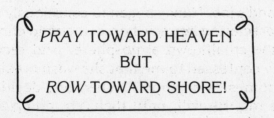

PRAY TOWARD HEAVEN
BUT
ROW TOWARD SHORE!

What is God's responsibility? To answer our prayers. And ours? To keep on rowing!

How much effort have we really put into improving our lives? Into bettering our relationships? Into reaching our goals? Dip those oars! Bend those elbows!

As you begin to move ahead, you may discover that God has calmed the sea, quieted the wind, and rebuked the angry storm. All of a sudden things don't seem so bad. Who knows? Maybe there's going to be a happy ending after all!

Chapter Ten

The Real Happy Ending

The big church was very still. Next on the program was the evening's special guest speaker. No one knew quite what to expect. In the momentary hush a wheelchair moved quietly across the stage. A beautifully dressed young woman, her eyes shining like stars was seated in the "invalid" conveyance. Then she began to speak.

Have you heard her for yourself? Her name is Joni. Years ago she lost the use of most of her body in a tragic diving accident. Today her smile is familiar to millions. She is a spokesperson for the handicapped, a symbol of victory over outrageous circumstances, and an outspoken witness to the love of Jesus.

In a case like Joni's, it's easy for us who gather at her feet to long for a miracle. "Why hasn't God healed her?" we ask ourselves. "What a story *that* would be!" Doubtless Joni has asked herself the same questions.

And she has probably been assaulted by the inquiries of those well-meaning Christians who are forever wondering, "Who's to blame?"

"She must have some kind of sin in her life or she'd be healed!" I can almost hear the judgmental tones of those discussing the "dilemma."

"It's hard to believe she's a real sinner—maybe she's just weak in her faith."

At times the Cinderella Syndrome thinking that infects Christians seems almost incurable. "Happy endings" get all tangled up with the miraculous. "Happily ever after" gets muddled with the "sweet by-and-by."

It's important for us to remember that even Lazarus, whom Jesus miraculously raised from the dead, *had to die again!* Clearly we are residents of an imperfect world.

As far as Joni herself is concerned, it's hard to find a better example of freedom from Cinderella Syndrome thinking. Here is a woman imprisoned by her own broken body. She is limited in ways that most of us "normal" types can't even imagine. And what is she doing about it? She is carving contentment out of crummy circumstances.

Joni's hands don't work too well. So she paints with a brush between her teeth—and she paints beautifully.

Joni can't walk. So she sings so tenderly, so touchingly, that no one can avoid being moved by her music. To hear a woman in her condition sing "Take my life and let it be consecrated, Lord, to Thee. . . Take my hands and let them move at the impulse of Thy love" is a life-changing moment.

Joni can't relate some miracle story about how strength returned to her crippled limbs. But she can share, like no one else, how God has poured spiritual vitality through her. And He has given her more than her share—enough to pass it on to countless others.

Those who hear her are often locked deeply in dungeons of their own minds. They are far less free than she is in her bright, open world of hope and reaching out.

Joni embodies many truths about glorious, contented living. But one truth in particular that we can all grasp involves *other people*. An excellent way to get our minds off our own haunting problems is to consider the needs of those around us.

The apostle Paul advised in Philippians 2:4, "Look not every man on his own things, but every man also on the things of others" (KJV). Could it be that out there in our neighborhoods, just down the street, maybe even next door, someone is having a more difficult time than we are?

You may long to reach out. I may have a great desire to help others. But until you and I get our own Cinderella Syndromes under control, we really don't have a whole lot to offer.

"So how about it—isn't there a happy ending at all? If God's got all that power, what's He going to do for *me*?" I've heard this question asked a thousand different ways by woman of every age, denomination, and personality.

Churches are full of folks smitten with the Cinderella Syndrome. They are waiting for the sweet by-and-by," ever avoiding the "nasty here-and-now."

Too often a kind of "pie-in-the-sky" theology only reinforces their holding pattern, robbing them of contentment. Some are fooled into waiting for their "ministry" to descend upon them. Others wait for a "divine healing." And a certain element is just "hanging in there, brother, until the Lord comes."

Make no mistake—I believe in gifts and ministries. I have witnessed divine healing, and I look forward joyously to the second coming of Jesus Christ. But I also know that God never intended that the *anticipation* of blessings should *paralyze* us. He isn't pleased to see us simply putting in our time until some provision finally arrives.

And I'm not a fairy godmother myself. Much as I'd like to, I have no magic wand which can transform our various circumstances. Worse yet, I'm fresh out of magic dust to scatter across our assorted problems. Apparently fairytale solutions are out of the question, no matter how much wishing we do. So what do we have to hold onto?

Precious Promises

Not to be confused with a genie, a wizard, or a celestial fortune cookie, our mighty God of all creation has made some incredible *promises* to us. And He, unlike the mortal created in His image, always does exactly what he says He'll do.

"You can count on me," smiled the squinty-eyed garage mechanic. But as I handed him my car keys I had that funny, uncomfortable feeling. *You're gonna get ripped off, Lee!* said my inner voice of experience.

People make promises so glibly today. And I'm sure I'm not the only one who has been disillusioned by unkept commitments. We have all laughed inside when we've heard—"Your check is in the mail."

"Yes, ma'am. The washer repairman will be there before noon."

"Of course. Your dry cleaning will be ready tomorrow. No problem."

Could it be that we've gotten a little gun-shy when it comes to trusting in the promises of God? Politicians lie. Friends betray. Husbands disappear. Preachers backslide. Who can we really count on?

When I was a young girl growing up in Philadelphia, I had some desperate needs in my life. I wasn't old in body, but I had seen and experienced some things that had wrinkled and grayed my spirit. By the time I was 17 I needed a fresh start.

Did you know that God has promised us this very thing? A new beginning is available to anyone who chooses to follow Him: "If anyone is in Christ, he is a new creation; old things have passed away; behold, all things have become new" (2 Corinthians 5:17 NKJV).

When my spirit was reborn, I started life all over—with a clean slate. As you know, troubles don't just go away. But I was changed. And through Christ's life within me, I was given strength to wrestle with handling my strangling circumstances.

As a young adult and a believer, I longed for my prince to come. Eventually he did. (But he had two children in the saddle with him!) As I've described earlier, my marriage opened out to mixed reviews. No husband on earth could have lived up to my expectations! But did you know that God Himself has promised to be a Husband to us? Even those who have lost a husband can rejoice in this:

> Fear not, for you will not be put to
>   shame;
> Neither feel humiliated, for you will not
>   be disgraced;
> But you will forget the shame of your
>   youth...
> *For your husband is your Maker,*
> *Whose name is the Lord of hosts...*
> For the Lord has called you,
> Like a wife forsaken and grieved in
>   spirit,

Even like a wife of one's youth when she
is rejected (Isaiah 54:4-6 NASB).

Those words should break through the gloom that clouds the heart of every unmarried or unhappily married woman. There is only one Prince who promised "never to leave you or forsake you" (Hebrews 13:5). Many an earthly prince who is no longer around once promised something similar. And he simply hasn't had the staying power that his "princess" hoped for.

But what if the prince isn't the principal problem? Perhaps it's the "fairy-godmother" fantasy that's the culprit in our lives—the hope for external intervention. And maybe we *have* done all we can do to make things better. Maybe the next *is* up to God. What kind of a Person are we turning to?

To Him who is able to do exceeding
abundantly beyond all that we ask or
think, according to the power that works
within us (Ephesians 3:20 NASB).

Where Is That Power?

How much power is that? Power enough to defeat our archenemy, Satan! Power enough to swallow up death in resurrection! God *is* able. Are you able to trust Him?

With a powerful guide like Him directing our steps, we needn't get bogged down in the marshy past. "When my spirit was overwhelmed within me," King David wrote, "Thou didst know my path" (Psalm 142:3 NASB). God has been with us all along. Did you know He was there? His love hasn't diminished once—not even a little! He's just waiting for us to love Him back.

One wise, silver-bearded prophet of God wrote centuries ago:

This I recall to my mind,
Therefore I have hope.
The Lord's lovingkindnesses indeed
     never cease,
For His compassions never fail.
They are new every morning;
Great is Thy faithfulness (Lamentations
     3:21-23 NASB).

That certainly covers the present. But Jeremiah had a couple more things to say that left no doubt about the future either.

"The Lord is my portion, says my soul.
"Therefore I have hope in Him."
The Lord is good to those who wait for
     Him,
To the person who seeks Him (Lamenta-
     tions 3:24,25 NASB).

The past, the present, and the future maybe more comfortable for you than the people you have to live with. Some of us just seem to crave the approval of others. We seemed to be virtually enslaved by their opinions.

Yet back in Bible times, there really were *slaves*. And certain promises were given even to them. It doesn't take much stretching to apply them to us, too:

> Slaves, in all things obey those who are your masters on earth, not with external service as those who merely please men, but with sincerity of heart, fearing the Lord. Whatever you do, do your work heartily, as for the Lord rather than for men, knowing that from the Lord you will receive the reward of the inheritance. It is the Lord Christ whom you serve (Colossians 3:22-24 NASB).

"No problem," you might say. "People are no problem. It's the tightrope-walking that's making me jittery." Take heart! We all sway and swing a little here and there, wondering where our responsibility ends and God's begins. And He's made a promise with regard to that delicate balance that bears repeating:

> If any of you lacks wisdom, let him ask of God, who gives to all men generously and without reproach, and it will be given to him (James 1:5 NASB).

Richer than the gold, silver, and precious gems that sparkle in the world's wealthiest vaults are the promises of God. And we are not paupers when it comes to our inheritance. "Every promise in the book is mine," says the old song. And nothing could be more true.

That pushy, windburned old fisherman, Peter, miraculously became a messenger of the kingdom of God by the power of the Holy Spirit. And through Peter God has made yet another vow to us:

> His divine power has granted to us everything pertaining to life and godliness, through the true knowledge of Him who called us by His own glory and excellence. For by these He has granted to us His precious and magnificent promises (2 Peter 1:3,4 NASB).

Great Gain

Did you catch that? *Everything* pertaining to life and godliness. Shouldn't this be enough to make us happy? Satisfied? Content? The Scripture encourages us that "great gain" can be had by any one of us. Its equation is defined as follows:

$$\begin{aligned} &\text{Godliness} \\ + &\underline{\text{Contentment}} \\ = &\text{Great Gain} \end{aligned}$$

1 Timothy 6:6

This passage of Scripture goes on to admonish us that "we brought nothing into this world, and it is certain we can carry nothing out . . . for the love of money is the root of all evil."

"Great gain" does not consist in tangible things, as we mentioned before. Jesus instructed us in Matthew 6 to "seek first the kingdom of God and His righteousness, and all these [tangible] things shall be added to you" (NKJV). The kingdom of God itself (according to Romans 14:17) is not "food and drink, but righteousness and peace, and joy" (NKJV).

The things that really count in our lives are not externals, such as a bigger house, a better job, or a beautiful man. Our wealth needs to lie in the *internals*—the riches of a holy, transformed spirit. Actually, the externals aren't meant to affect us much at all, one way or the other.

Suppose a woman accepts Christ on Sunday evening. Monday morning she wakes up with the flu. "Thanks a lot, God!" She mutters. "This is *not* what I signed up for!"

Oh, really? Check the fine print in 2 Corinthians 4:8!

> We are troubled on every side—yet not distressed;
> We are perplexed—but not in despair;
> We are persecuted—but not forsaken;
> We are cast down—but not destroyed;
> We are always bearing in the body the dying of the Lord Jesus,

So that the life of Jesus might be made
manifest in our body!

What God has in mind is not to protect us from
problems that could make us discontent. Instead,
He wants to *lead us through* heavy trials, through
difficulties that have the potential of crushing us.
In this way He shows us that His strength is
sufficient.

[God said unto me], "My power shows
up best in *weak* people." Now I am glad
to boast about how weak I am; I am glad
to be a living demonstration of Christ's
power, instead of showing off my *own*
power and abilities. . . the less I have,
the more I depend on Him (2 Corinthians 12:9,10 TLB).

Custom Made Circumstances

The splintery, rugged situation in which you
find yourself has been custom-made by a Master
Carpenter just for you. It is intended to strip you
of trust in yourself!

Obviously the apostle Paul had discovered all
this when he wrote from his jail cell in Philippians
4:11-13, "Not that I speak from want, for I have
learned to be content in whatever circumstance
I am. I know how to get along with humble
means, and I also know how to live in prosperity; in any and every circumstance I have learned
the secret of being filled and going hungry, both

of having abundance and suffering need. For I can do all things through Him who strengthens me" (NASB).

Our satisfaction is unconditionally guaranteed. But it is not contained in some glass slipper which we are anxiously awaiting. Our genuine possessions are to be found in Christ, and can be discovered within us *now*, in our *present* state of affairs.

There was never a freer man than Paul, dragging heavy chains around his prison cell. There was never a freer woman than Joni, physically limited as she is.

What has us locked up today? What cripples us? Maybe it's a person who won't cooperate. Or an illness. Or a stubborn, resisting child. Or a checkbook full of red ink.

The jailed apostle chose to make the most of his "shackled" state. And in the inner liberty he felt, Paul wrote in Philippians 1:14:

> Because of my imprisonment many of
> the Christians here seem to have lost
> their fear of chains! (TLB).

Isn't that wonderful? And wouldn't it be exciting if other people, looking at the situation which limits us most, could see our freedom and grace? Perhaps they too would lose their fear of "chains" after seeing what Christ has done!

Tradition tells us that one day the great violinist Paganini was getting prepared to walk onto the stage for a concert. He reached for his priceless Stradivarius in its plush velvet case. To his horror he found that it had been stolen! In its place lay a secondhand, beat-up fiddle.

On the other side of the curtain the audience roared. Unaware of his shocking discovery, they were breathlessly anticipating his entrance. Paganini calmly picked up the battered violin, with two of its four strings missing. Confidently he went to center stage.

Before he began to play, the master announced that his fine instrument had been taken. He explained that another violin, much in need of repair, had been left in its place.

"Nevertheless," he smiled, "I shall play the concerto. I would like to prove to you that music is not in the *instrument*. Music is in the *soul!*" It is said that one of his finest performances followed.

You may be missing a string or two. I may be sadly in need of tuning. We may both be carved of flawed, unresonant wood. But what kind of music are we playing?

"Someday my prince will come"?

"Yesterday all my troubles seemed so far away"?

"Is that all there is"?

"Tomorrow, tomorrow, I'll love you tomorrow"?

God has carefuly composed the heartlifting song of the lark, the whispered lullaby of the wind, the thundering chorus of the ocean tides.

And He has placed a new song in the heart of every true believer in His Son, Jesus. But it's no shallow musical comedy score, no dull rehash of "oldies but goodies," no futile fairytale theme.

By now we've practiced blending the past, the present, and the future into an agreeable harmony. We've learned that happiness is a solo performance. We've trained ourselves to feel the complex counterpoint rhythm that weaves God's purposes into our plans.

But don't expect a Hallelujah Chorus finale. There will be no resounding, concluding "Amen." God's eloquent compositions play on and on.

Like your ongoing story. Like my continuing journey.

Like life itself, the believer's song has no happy ending. How could it end? Jesus has promised us eternity! "We've only just begun . . ."